praise for *Bringing Bubb*

"This courageous, poignant, and truthful book will give you an experience that will never leave you. You will become wiser in the reading, shocked and compassionate as love rises to the challenge of tending to life's end."

—Jean Houston, author of *A Mythic Life*

"Heartfelt and often humorous, *Bringing Bubbe Home* offers a keen and compassionate account of the love, dread, exhaustion, devotion, and revelation that come when Zaslow opens her home and her heart to her dying grandmother. With the true talent of a storyteller, Debra Zaslow takes us on a journey of self-doubt, self-discovery, and, finally, reconciliation as she explores what it means to remember . . . and to be remembered."

—Kim Barnes, author of *In the Wilderness*

"Unable to bear seeing her Russian-born, 103-year-old grandmother die in a nursing home, Zaslow makes the decision to care for her during her final months. *Bringing Bubbe Home* is deeply compassionate, but unflinching. This book chronicles the realities of the body, the demands of our emotions, and the promise of the spirit. The beauty here is hard-won and authentic."

—Sue William Silverman, author of *Love Sick*

"Debra Zaslow offers insightful and poignant perspectives on family relationships. She has a natural ear for dialogue and captures the dynamics of taking care of an elder, her grandmother, along with taking care of the teenage children in the same home. Reading the memoir made me feel part of the entire experience!

"Zaslow profoundly sums it all up near the end of her memoir, 'The past and present travel with us, tracing parallel lines . . . . My roots are still tangled in Bubbe's past, the edges forever blurred.' What they lived through remains in my sense memory as I traveled with Zaslow and her Bubbe.

Bringing Bubbe Home, a form of an 'Ethical Will,' is a beautiful tribute to her Bubbe and the wisdom learned that can be transmitted through the generations."

–Peninnah Schram, author of *Jewish Stories One Generation Tells Another*

"Debra Zaslow takes us on an intimate journey, as profound as it is warm-hearted and full of nourishment for the soul. You may find yourself laughing and crying at once, and tucking away seeds of wisdom for future use."

–Rabbi Tirzah Firestone, author of *With Roots in Heaven* and *The Receiving: Reclaiming Jewish Women's Wisdom*

"*Bringing Bubbe Home*, is full of wisdom, humor, love, and the reality and comfort of family. I loved everything about it."

–Ruth Bell Alexander, co-author of *Our Bodies Ourselves*, principal author of *Changing Bodies, Changing Minds*

"This book presents a raw, loving, intimate glimpse into the world of critical home caregiving. Swirling through the experience are dense layers of family dynamics, memories, and traumas reaching back generations. Debra Gordon Zaslow, is courageous, conflicted, caring, loving, joyful, and exhausted. Readers will be drawn into the world of personal caregiving and its ramifications upon all our lives."

–Cherie Karo Schwartz, storyteller and author of *Circle Spinning: Jewish Turning and Returning Tales*

"*Bringing Bubbe Home* becomes impossible to put down. Necessary truths and family secrets are revealed in the mature voice of a world-class storyteller. I immediately told friends to read this with the intent of a deep discussion. *Bringing Bubbe Home* is brilliantly confrontational, leading us to know ourselves and ask, 'Could we?' and 'Should we?'"

–Rabbi Goldie Milgram, co-editor of *Mitzvah Stories: Seeds for Inspiration and Learning*

A Memoir of Letting Go
Through Love and Death

Bringing Bubbe Home

A Memoir of Letting Go
Through Love and Death

Bringing Bubbe Home

Debra Gordon Zaslow

White Cloud Press
Ashland, Oregon

White Cloud Press books may be purchased for educational, business, or sales promotional use. For information, please write: Special Market Department, White Cloud Press, PO Box 3400, Ashland, OR 97520
Website: www.whitecloudpress.com

Cover and Interior Design by C Book Services

First edition: 2014

Printed in the United States of America

14 15 16 17 18   10 9 8 7 6 5 4 3 2 1

Library of Congress Cataloging-in-Publication Data

Zaslow, Debra Gordon.
Bringing Bubbe home : a memoir of letting go through love and death / by Debra Gordon Zaslow.
pages cm
ISBN 978-1-940468-02-0 (paperback)
1. Zaslow, Debra Gordon. 2. Granddaughters--United States--Biography. 3. Caregivers--United States--Biography. 4. Grandmothers--United States--Biography. 5. Jews--United States--Biography. 6. Grandparent and child--United States. 7. Older people--Care--United States. 8. Grandmothers--United States--Death. 9. Death--Psychological aspects. 10. Loss (Psychology) I. Title.
CT275.Z37A3 2014
306.874'5--dc23
2014003058

PART I
Waterfall

Energy released in the movement from a higher plane to a lower plane.
You have arrived at a place of sacrifice and return,
a place where bodhisattvas bathe.

–Earth Voices Deck, Robert Beridha

one

November 1, 1996

Do not bother me in the morning. Not unless it is life or death.

A simple rule for the children of a late sleeper.

Later in the day I'll help my kids with homework, mediate disputes, or drive them to places they could walk to in five minutes, but in the morning they've learned to scramble an egg and walk to school with friends while I drowse.

This morning when my fourteen-year-old daughter, Rachel, opens my bedroom door at seven am, I know it's important. I roll over in bed and squint at the outline of her long brown hair as she leans in. "Peaky died," she says. He's the little green parakeet she's had for eight years. We've been expecting this for a few weeks since he's been wobbling on his perch, shedding so many feathers that his coat is a pale, mottled gray. I sit up in bed.

"Did you cry?"

She shakes her head. "No."

When I walk into her room and see Peaky lying rigid on the bottom of his cage, *I* cry. It's not that Peaky was so loveable; he always pecked our fingers and never liked to be handled. But now his jumbled chatter is so absent that the whole room feels empty. I begin to pray silently for his spirit to soar—an appropriate response for a *rebbitzin* and apt for a bird. But I know that I'm also praying that there is spirit beyond body and that when I lie cold in the bottom of my cage there will be somewhere for my soul to fly.

David, my husband, gently wraps Peaky in a newspaper, so Rachel can bury him later. He slides the newspaper bundle into a bag that he labels with black felt pen, "Peaky Zaslow," then places the package on our back porch overlooking the Siskiyou Mountains.

The next day I sit on our deck watching Stellar Jays dip and swoop, their wings deep blue against the gray November sky, while Rachel buries Peaky under the redwood tree in the yard below. Ari, our twelve-year-old, has reluctantly agreed to help her, since I think it would be a good brother-sister project. Their voices mix with the shrieking and nattering of the Jays.

"NO, Ari! Not there! Dig on this side."

"I can't. There's too many rocks."

"Just do it where I say! It's my bird!"

"You want my help or not?"

"No! Give me the shovel!"

I hear Rachel scrape the earth as Ari climbs onto the trampoline. His head bounces into view, his blond hair flapping up, then vanishing. Rachel mutters, her shovel clanks; her brother sails up, floats down.

I watch as if through a blurred lens, wanting to nudge them into focus. The older they get, the busier we are, rushing in every direction, being testy with one another. I know enough not to interfere in everything they do, but I push down a sour taste in my mouth, a gnawing sense that if I could just adjust the camera, the picture would sharpen, emerge flawless. Rewind: *Bury Peaky with dignity, treat each other kindly. Stop for a minute. Breathe in the smell of death, the fresh earth, breathe out sadness.*

That evening I sit down and draw a card from my "Earth Voices" deck, sort of like Tarot cards with a nature theme. I'm not somebody who throws the "I Ching," or has my palm read, but David describes me as a solid realist with a mystical bent. He says, "If someone asked you if you believed in angels, you'd say, 'Of course not,' but if they asked you if you *talked* to angels, you'd say, 'All the time.'"

I draw "Waterfall": *Movement from a higher plane to a lower plane . . . You have arrived at a place of sacrifice and return. A place where bodhisattvas bathe.* This sounds monumental, but I don't know what it has to do with me. Strange, this same card has surfaced three times in the past month. I asked David, "Why do I keep getting this message?"

He shrugged. "There just must be a lot of Waterfall cards in the deck."

I finger the card slowly, turn it over and place it deliberately back in the center of the deck.

Three days later, as I vacuum the last bits of feathery dust and seed husks from Rachel's carpet, David calls. He's in Los Angeles for a weekend rabbinic conference.

"What's the address of Bubbe's nursing home?"

I turn off the vacuum cleaner. "You want to visit Bubbe?" She's my 103 year-old grandmother who has been in nursing home for a year and a half. "You hate hospitals."

David remembers squirming under a mask of cold ether when his tonsils were taken out at three years old. He's avoided being a patient in the forty-six years since then, but after he became a rabbi a few years ago he's had to steel himself to visit sick congregants. He hates to walk down the scrubbed hallways with pale faces peering from behind curtains, and nurses make him edgy, as if they have hypodermic needles hidden behind their starched smiles. Bubbe's in a nursing home, but it has all the trappings of a hospital, with an added air of decay.

"I'm so close," David says, "and I haven't seen her in the home."

It's strange to have to look up my grandma's address since she lived in the same house for forty years. In her nineties when I'd call and ask how she was, she'd reply, "Gettin' old, honey, gettin' old." After she reached a hundred, she'd answer, "Not so good, honey. It's da old age. Da old age is here to stay." I pictured her serving a life sentence in her white stucco house in the San Fernando Valley, with the old age clinging to her like a heavy hump.

Just before she turned one hundred and two, a fall landed her in the hospital, bruised and disoriented. My aunt Minnie, her oldest daughter, announced, "The doctor says she can't live alone anymore." To Minnie, doctors are like God, and this was the final verdict.

"So what if the doctor says that!" I countered, "She *wants* to go home. She should live her last years wherever she wants to be." My sisters and I suggested that Minnie and Aunt Derril get her live-in care, but the cost was astronomical. The choices were slim on such short notice, so Minnie found a Jewish retirement home in a row of indistinguishable faded buildings, a colorless, depressing "old-folks home," just where Bubbe didn't want to end up.

I call David back to give him the address. "Give Bubbe a hug for me," I tell him, but I know she may not remember me now.

The first time Rachel and I visited the home a year ago Bubbe was still alert. We pulled up to the faded pink building where a few old people, hunched in wheelchairs, were positioned on the porch, like gargoyles at the gate. The odor in the hallway was *Eau de Nursing Home*: A blend of equal parts urine, disinfectant, and decay. At the door marked "Lena Kanter," we peeked in to see Bubbe sitting on a folding chair by the bed, wearing rumpled stretch pants and a loose flowered blouse that was too lively for her grim, lined face. It looked as if she had been plunked down into a worn-out doll's house where all the furniture was just a little out of scale.

"HI, GRANDMA!" I hollered. Her eyes widened as we walked in.

"HI, BUBBE!" Rachel knelt by her chair. My sisters and cousins grew up calling her Grandma, but her great-grandchildren call her Bubbe.

"Vell, look who's here—Rachel!" She remembered her even though she hadn't seen her in over a year.

We took a walk in the hall where we passed her neighbors, peering from their wheelchairs. Bubbe nodded to me and whispered, "Dese are da old folks."

When my sister Nancy, who had picked us up at the airport, went in the bathroom, Bubbe leaned into me and wrinkled her nose. "Ven did Nentsy put on so much vait?" I felt like smacking her, so I knew she was still her old self.

Before we left I sat and held her hand. "Do you want to go home, Bubbe?"

"Dey say I kent go home. Vat ken I do?"

A few months ago, when we visited again, it was a different story. Rachel and I tiptoed into the room to find Bubbe curled up on the bed snoring, clutching the bedclothes in both fists, as if she might slide off on to the floor. The stink of urine was so thick we had to hold our breath. Hearing us, she sat up in bed and squinted like a confused child woken from a nap. The last year had shriveled her, as if in an accelerated time-lapse, into another creature. Without dentures or glasses, her jaw jutted out under hollow cheeks and her eyes looked vacant and filmy. Her hair, which had always been in tidy, sensible ringlets, stuck out in wild greasy strands.

Aunt Minnie had recently hired a private attendant to give round the clock care, since Bubbe had become too disoriented to care for herself, but there was no one in sight. I called the front desk and a moment later the attendant walked in, nodded to us, strode over to the bed, and yanked off Bubbe's nightgown. She sat in the middle of the bed, one hundred and three years old, naked, blinking like a wrinkled baby bird in the nest. Rachel looked away as Bubbe smiled sheepishly, her thin arms fumbling to cover her chest. I stepped forward, as if to defend her, felt words rising in my throat, *For God's sake! Allow her some dignity!* Instead I stepped back and smiled into Bubbe's eyes, nodding reassuringly as if this were perfectly normal. The nurse grabbed a dress, pulled Bubbe's arms through the tight armholes, and jerked it over her head. She emerged, looking ashamed. The attendant slapped new sheets on the bed, stroked them smooth, and marched out.

Rachel sat down on the bed, leaned into Bubbe and kissed her gently. "HOW ARE YOU, BUBBE?" she asked.

"Oy, honey, not so good," Bubbe answered in a gravelly whisper. "Da old age is here to stay."

When David gets back from Los Angeles we stand in the kitchen as he tells me about his visit to the nursing home. Bubbe stared at him as he walked into her room. He was ordained as a rabbi in Jewish Renewal, a branch of Judaism that blends old rituals with modern practices, which is kind of how he looks. He has the beard and yarmulke of a Hassidic rabbi, but the yarmulke is crocheted purple and green, and he wears it with a pair of jeans and a plaid flannel shirt. Bubbe didn't recognize that it was David, whom she adores, but she nodded and said, "The Rebbi came to see me." She took his hand and kneaded it for the next hour, murmuring to him in a rush of Yiddish. David doesn't understand Yiddish, but he understood the stroking.

We're silent for a moment, picturing the scene, feeling the pull of her gnarled hand. I lean against the kitchen counter as David peers at me, his dark eyes magnified by his glasses. "We have to bring her here," he says. "We can't leave her to die there." I nod, speechless. David puts his arm around my shoulder and we stand there, nodding, like dolls on a car dashboard going over a slow bump.

In the night I wake with a stabbing pain in my back, between my shoulder blades, all the way through to my ribs, connected to my heart. I try to go back to sleep, but a voice that waits for the dark announces, *You are insane to bring your grandmother here! Living with teenagers is enough! This will be way too stressful for you to handle. Get real!* The voice has a point, but I don't want to listen. This, I figure, must be the "Place of Sacrifice and Return."

two

The next day we sit down with the kids to talk about Bubbe coming. Ari leans back in his chair, brushes his bleached blond hair off his forehead, and says, "Sure, okay, Bubbe can come. Can I fly first class with you to get her? I've never flown first class. *Please*, can I?"

"Would you be willing to spend some time with her?" I ask.

"Well, yeah, sure, if I'm not busy." He rocks in the chair a little, tipping his head.

"How do you feel about us bringing her here to die?"

"No problem," he says." I've seen Papa Sam dead. But I puked."

Papa Sam is David's father, who died two years ago. David and Ari were with him in Miami in his last days.

I turn to Rachel who sits straight up in her chair, glaring at me. She spends every Sunday visiting old folks in the local nursing home instead of hanging out with her friends at the mall, so I assumed she'd be eager to apply her generosity at home, the opportunity for the *mitzvah* of a lifetime. But she just stares and shakes her head. "It's going to be really hard," she says." Harder than you think." I know she's right. She sees through me like the voice in the night, sees that my heart can stretch too far and come up empty, knows that I'll be overwhelmed.

I'm the only one in my extended family who's willing and able to do this right now. Bubbe has outlived three of her five children. My mother, her middle daughter, died of cancer twenty-one years ago. Her two remaining daughters, Minnie and Derril, and her eleven grandchildren all have mixed feelings about her. She was a peasant from Russia who'd had a tough life, a worrier whose grim warnings and hand wringing tugged on our modern, carefree lives. Bubbe would say tearfully, "I love you," and in the next moment scowl and tell you that you'd die of "kenser" if you didn't eat your vegetables. My mother and aunts were always tense around her, as if she tripped a switch that made their cheeks flush and their eyes harden, ready for defense.

I do my share of *mitzvahs*, or good deeds, but I don't sacrifice. I volunteer in my kids' classrooms, bring the occasional pot of chicken soup to a sick friend, and hand dollars to the homeless at freeway ramps, but I don't invite them to come home with me. This is definitely going to be a stretch.

I stare back at Rachel. "I know," I tell her. "It's going to be hard."

Rachel says what she really wants is a puppy. Ari says he'd rather have a cute little Indian baby like our friends the Levys adopted, but it looks like that's not what's coming to the Zaslows.

As soon as David and I sit down to organize Bubbe's move, we start to bicker about how much work it will take to transfer her life in less than two weeks. We have to haul his office equipment into my office, order hospital furniture and supplies, convert his office into a mini-nursing home for Bubbe and the caretakers, whom we have yet to hire, wade through Medicare paperwork, set up hospice support, and deal with nervous relatives.

"Just a day or two of stuff to do," David says. "I did it for my dad."

"You did not bring your dad into *our* home." Three years ago when he flew back and forth to Florida to be with his dying father, he and his brother hired professional caregivers in the last months.

"True, I didn't bring him here." David drums his fingers on his desk. "But there was plenty to arrange, and it didn't take that much time."

"I'm trying to get everything set up so it will work!"

" Stop being such a perfectionist."

"I have no choice," I tell him. "I *am* a perfectionist, and furthermore, I'm right. *You* are in denial."

I stomp down the stairs to my office, where I sit on the floor, gazing around, as if searching for someone to help me. The shelves are lined with folktales of strong women, my specialty as a professional storyteller. When I started telling stories in schools and libraries fifteen years ago, I began to search for tales of women who were more than swooning beauties waiting to be rescued. I've found heroines with wit, spunk, and courage to fill my repertoire, so now the women in my audience have someone to cheer on.

It goes both ways. When I rehearse, I picture those hardy maidens and fierce witches guiding me through the stories and I come out feeling stronger. My office is adorned with females. A wooden angel with a *shofar* gazes at me; a mermaid clock ticks; on the coffee table a Guatemalan doll gives birth, surrounded by cloth women. Today, though, instead of lending me courage, they just stare back. I wish I could see the shape of the true story I'm about to walk into, but there are no guides for what lies ahead. I feel as alone today as Bubbe lying in her bed in the nursing home. Small and lonely.

I glance up to see Rachel making her way downstairs. From the minute she was born she had the air of an adult with a strong purpose, for whom childhood was an annoyance. When she was seven she led her friends in her own Passover Seder. At nine she started a school-wide ecology program, in middle school she ran her own summer camp for kids, and now she's the only freshman in the high school social-action theatre troop. Since she's only fourteen, she can't drive herself to any of her engagements, but she's good at organizing me into her plans.

Rachel is breathless. "Mom, I need a ride to Kate's—we're going to make vegetable soup to take to the nursing home, and can I use your phone first?"

"No, I need my space here. Use the upstairs phone."

"Mom, I just need a minute. What is *wrong* with you?" She gives me the hard stare that teenage girls reserve for their mothers.

"I just need my space," I repeat dumbly.

Rachel looks at me squarely, takes a breath, walks over, and hugs me. "So, you're worried about Bubbe coming." She settles down next to me on the floor and leans over until our heads tip into each other. I cannot hide from my daughter.

When Rachel leaves, I lie down on the futon for a moment, trying to relax, but images of my grandmother keep floating through my mind. I remember standing on the porch at her house in North Hollywood, a pale stucco box with a dying lawn. I could always feel her waiting inside. No matter what time we arrived we'd already hurt her feelings. She thought we were coming an hour ago, the chicken was overcooked and the rice pudding was getting cold.

My parents and my sisters and I would listen to the sounds of the locks and latches jostling and snapping. When Grandma finally opened the door I'd have to lower my gaze to find her. She was barely five feet, compact and sturdy with large, solid breasts. "Oy, I look terrible," she'd say. "I put on a house dress." She announced this as if there were a closetful of other options, but her few dresses were all indistinguishable, faded, sturdy cotton.

Grandma's hair was in tight, thinning, gray ringlets. It seemed to lose ground each year, revealing more scalp, just as the hairbrush she kept in the bathroom lost bristles each year. I would always open the drawer when I went in her bathroom, to stare at the brush and finger it, like a strange foreign relic. It had more black stubble each year where bristles had broken off, leaving clogged empty pores. When she turned one hundred years old, she would still have it, with six thin bristles remaining.

Her face was grim, but welcoming. She was, of course, happy to see us, but then again we were so late and she looked so awful and the food was cold. She dabbed at her eyes, then rung her hands. I had to kiss my grandma, but I never really wanted to. Her cheeks felt warm and furry, like a decaying peach. I was drawn to their deep softness, their etched lines, but I was also repelled.

In the morning David begins moving into my office so Bubbe and her caregivers can occupy his office. *You have arrived at the place of Sacrifice and Return. Can I turn back? Do not pass Go. Do not go to the Place where Bodhisattvas Bathe. You could drown.*

Years ago this was David's office, a cluttered L-shaped den where he wrote poetry and ran his business ventures before he became a rabbi. When my storytelling career was taking off, I moved in to share his office. With me rehearsing out loud, though, practicing dialogue, gestures and intonation, over and over, it wasn't easy to share a small space.

David (on the phone): Where would you like the books sent?

Me (voice booming): Deep in a dark forest where no flowers grew...

David (cupping his hand over his ear): How shall I send them?

Me (arms flying): On horseback, with long hair flowing, the maiden rode through the night.

David: Thanks; I'll have them sent UPS today.

After a year of that, we tore down a wall and added enough square feet to transform the office into a large, airy space for both of us. As we moved back in, I grumbled while David hauled in his old furniture and piles of equipment. "NO! Do not put that there! That's *my* shelf! Do you have keep *every* book from college twenty years ago?"

"Just take this office for yourself," David sighed. "I'll use part of the family room."

It took me a week to convince myself that I deserved a room of my own. When I asked David if he was serious he said, "Yes, take it, but only on the condition that you don't ever tell me where to put anything in *my* office."

In the next months I chose each piece of furniture and artwork as if I were decorating the holiest temple. *My* colors, *my* shapes, *my* books. David, ever able to adapt, set up his desk in the family room, made himself a new cluttered nest, and hunkered down to work. It's here in my office, tucked away under our house, that I weave new stories, try out voices, speak to my ancestors, dance, pray, be alone, be alive, be myself.

Now, as we move David's things in, it feels like a slo-mo version of *Invasion of the Body Snatchers*, my insides quietly being replaced by alien parts, one by one. David leans to open the sliding-glass door to the office. His computer printer is tucked under one arm and there are cords stuffed into various pockets poking out. He has to duck to miss the hanging lamp as he deposits the printer on the table. His curly hair spews out the sides of his yarmulke; the top is flat, a little like Bozo the clown. Rachel claims he became a rabbi just so he could cover up his expanding bald spot with a hat.

I sit on the floor, wrestling two telephones, yanking at the cords, trying to sort out the connections so both lines work in one room. I glower at David, jerk the cords out, and toss the phones into the corner. "I can't do this!"

David turns to retrieve another load.

I stand up. "Don't go."

"What's the matter?" He looks at me warily as I walk over and put my hands on his shoulders.

"I feel like I'm falling apart."

"Look, I'm doing everything I can." His body stiffens. "I'm exhausted, too. I just led a huge Bat Mitzvah yesterday."

"I need more support."

"Why don't you just relax?"

"That is a very good question."

David peers down at me. He's six-foot-two and as he squints out of his glasses, I can see that his eyes are tired. "I just need to take care of myself today," he repeats. It always annoys me that he can state his needs so easily. No fanfare.

"I just need you, too, you cold bastard." We laugh. We hug. We've been here before. I know he can only do what he can do, but I ache for more.

I want my family to cover me like a blanket the way they did when we were on the way to Canada last summer. It had been ten years since I'd seen my disabled sister, JoAnn, and my feelings about her were growing more ambivalent as we approached the border. In the back seat, I began to cry quietly, and Ari, next to me, said, "What's wrong, Mom?"

I whispered, "I'm scared to go see my sister."

He reached out his hand and said tenderly, "It's okay, Mom."

From the front seat, Rachel turned and gently handed me a Kleenex. David reached back as he drove, put his hand on mine, and a sweet calm settled around us, in sharp contrast to the bickering that often fills our car on long trips. It was soft and simple, like being wrapped in an old, warm afghan.

I want that afghan now. We're not on a car trip, but we're quietly speeding toward an unknown destination. I want to tell David, *I'm scared.* I've invited Bubbe, but I can't control what's coming my way. *It's old; it leaks traces of poison, smells of fear and old rust.* I don't know how to say this though, so we go on rearranging the furniture.

three

Marilyn, a member of our congregation who has done some nursing care, comes over to talk about being the main caregiver. Even though we've calculated that Bubbe's round-the-clock care will be expensive, we know we can't do it ourselves. When our babies were new I wanted to stay home and was young enough to haul myself out of bed at night to nurse and still be able get up in the morning to make breakfast. Now, at forty-five I know my limits. Even if I wanted to be up at night with Bubbe, I'd be too worn out to work the next day. It's a lot harder, though, to find babysitters for an elder.

Marilyn is an ample, warm woman in her late fifties with long, thick graying hair, and she peers carefully around the room that has just been cleared of David's things.

"This is where Bubbe will sleep." I show her the space under the window. "The hospital bed should arrive in the next few days."

"And where would I sleep?"

"This couch opens up." As Marilyn sits down on the old Naugahyde sofa bed and frowns, I realize I'm going to be responsible for the comfort of more people than I'd expected. We talk about Bubbe's condition, her growing tumor, what food she might eat. We have to yell intermittently over the pounding of the handyman who is installing support rails for Bubbe by the toilet and in the tub. BANG, TAP, BANG!

"How much are you planning to pay?" Marilyn's question rises easily over the din, and I note her strong voice will be the perfect volume for Bubbe. When I tell her the figure we've arrived at for each twenty-four hour shift, she wrinkles her eyebrows. "I'd hoped to get more."

"I wish we could afford more, but Medicare doesn't cover home care and that's the most we can manage for full-time care." TAP, TAP, PING.

Marilyn says nothing, so I go on loudly as if I'm selling something, "You'll probably be sleeping for eight of the hours and we'll be supplying all your food." The hammering stops, but I'm still shouting. "SO IT MIGHT NOT BE SUCH A BAD DEAL!"

Marilyn scans the room, pokes a Naugahyde cushion. "Well, I don't know."

Suddenly I feel sort of sleazy, like we're trying to take advantage of a poor woman. Aunt Minnie, who will be footing most of the bill with some help from Aunt Derril, has been paying for the retirement home. This morning when I told her home care would cost twice as much, she declared, "That's prohibitive." David and I have decided it won't prohibit us. We'll put out the extra money from our savings and hope that it's re-imbursed when Bubbe's house is sold. She's not expected to live more than six months, but you never know. I show Marilyn a photo of Bubbe, and she smiles. She agrees to let me know in a few days.

What I hadn't foreseen in all of this preparation was speaking to practically every member of my family six times a day. Since nobody ever says what they mean, I have to decode the messages.

> Relative number one, on the answering machine: (in an energetic, but long-suffering voice): "Well I've been trying to call you back, but first the line was busy for ages and now there's no one answering. . ."
>
> Meaning: *"As usual, no one loves me or cares about me as much as I need. I'm still hurt and angry with you because you didn't come see me last time you were in town, not to mention all I suffered as a child."*
>
> Relative number two, when I return her call in the daytime and ask if she can talk: (tone of voice as if she is talking to a very young child who isn't too bright): "Oh, nooo, I'm *working*. I can't talk now."

Meaning: *"I am angry with you for not letting me know about this decision beforehand. I like to be consulted about everything and give lots of strong opinions. Just because I lie in bed all day doesn't mean I don't have an important life. I will have to be busy when you call so I can get back at you and put things in my control by manipulation."*

Relative number three: "Have you lost your mind?"

Meaning: *Have you lost your mind?*

Have I lost my mind? My life revolves around my kids, my husband, and my work, while I keep my extended family where they belong, just on the edges of my consciousness. Even when I was a child, it made my whole family anxious to have my grandma come over. Now she's not just coming over, she's moving in.

I'm seven years old. My grandparents have driven to our house to show us Grandpa's new creamy yellow '58 Chevy, with glossy chrome trim. The San Fernando Valley heat rises off the sleek fins, as we stand at the curb and marvel.

My parents and sisters and I look like any suburban family. With our hot pink shorts, sandals and sunglasses, you could match us up with any of the tract houses in "Storybook Lane," where the floor plans repeat every fourth house. My grandparents do not fit. Grandpa is sweaty in his rumpled wool trousers and long-sleeved shirt, while Grandma wears a worn print dress with a handkerchief tucked into the bosom. After his old Ford truck stopped running, Grandpa has bought the only new car they will ever own.

Grandma never approves of anything he does, but this extravagance has her really steamed. My grandpa, a solid man with a perpetual smirk and breath that smells of old cigars, shows us each feature, letting us touch the white vinyl upholstery, roll up and down the windows, and switch on the radio to KRLA Top-40, while Grandma grumbles.

"Our legs vil *stick* to dat seat in dis heat," she says, as if it were a slow death by a tropical disease. We ignore her, and continue exploring the new Chevy.

"If he plays da radio ven vere driving, ve'll get in an eccident." When no one responds, she adds, "Dat'll be da end of us."

When we all cram in for a test-drive, Grandma turns back to the house. My father leans out the window, "Come on, Ma, squeeze in with us." He calls her Ma, even though she's my mom's mother, and he never raises his voice to her no matter how irritating she gets. I figure this is because he's not related to her by blood. Everyone in her immediate family is annoyed by her, as though she were a raw prickle just under the skin.

Grandma glances back, her eyes widen, and I see the flicker of a half-smile on her face. It would be fun, wouldn't it, to squeeze in with your grandchildren in a new, yellow Chevy and careen around block with the radio blaring? Just for a lark? I think that's what I see on her face, but then she reaches her hand up, smoothes her hair and adjusts her face into a scowl, "Youse kids go if you vant. Hev a good time."

Later in the day, after lunch, my best friend, Bonnie, comes over to see if I can play. I'm about to race out the door when Grandma calls, "Vere are you going?"

"Out to ride bikes."

"You just ate," she declares. "You desn't go till you digest."

"That's *swimming*, Grandma, that can give you cramps," I explain. "We're just bike riding, and besides, I didn't eat much anyway."

"So, you couldn't take time to eat a helty lunch?"

"I *am* healthy, Grandma." I glance at the screen door. Bonnie stands on the porch, out of Grandma's view, mimicking, her arms raised like claws, her teeth bared. "EAT HELTY," she hisses, then clutches her side, giggling.

"I gotta go." I try to keep a straight face.

"You should take a jecket. You'll get cold."

"It's hot out," I say feebly, knowing it's useless to argue. Bonnie is doing a polar bear imitation on the porch, shivering. "Only NINETY DEGREES today under all this FUR," she growls.

"Anyway, exercise is healthy for me, Grandma! I'll see you later!"

Grandma nods, but I see she's planning on having the last word, "If you dunt get da exxersize, honey, you'll get fet, like your modder."

I slam the door. Bonnie is waddling on the porch, her hands in a huge circle around her fake girth. "OY VEY, I VISH I HED GOT SUM EXXERSIZE," she moans.

I hear my mother's voice, loud and shrill, from inside. I can't hear what she's saying, but I know she heard Grandma say she's fat and now they're going to go at it.

As we push our bikes down the driveway. Bonnie, still giggling, says, "God, your grandma's weird, isn't she?"

"I guess so." I hop onto my bicycle and start to pedal hard. Bonnie passes me quickly, her hair flapping behind her like a flag. She balances on her seat, then shoots both hands out to her sides.

"Look, Ma, no hands!" she screams.

I hold on tight to both handlebars. If I let go, I know I will fall.

four

This morning I look out the window to see the bright scarlet leaves of our dogwood tree have blown all over the driveway as fall slips toward winter. In the six days left until we pick up Bubbe, I'm trying to get everything ready while still teaching storytelling at the middle school. I have to be there early today so I scurry around looking for matching socks while gobbling a granola bar as Ari hollers at Rachel.

"It's your turn to walk Charlie!"

"No. It's your turn. Look at the chart!" Last week they scratched out a schedule that hangs on the refrigerator.

"Remember, you traded with me." I can almost see Ari's smug smile.

"Oh shit. Nicole will be here in five minutes. Mom! Can I walk Charlie after school?"

"No, he has to get out to pee. Take him around the block now and you can walk him longer after school."

Rachel whirls around as I walk into the kitchen. She wears fashionably ragged blue jeans and a velour leopard-print top that suits her dark, almond eyes and mane of thick, black hair. She howls at me, "I can't do everything! It's too much!"

I nod. "Boy, do I know what you mean."

Rachel sighs and grabs the dog leash. Charlie, who's been watching with one eye from under the kitchen table, leaps up and makes a dash to the front door.

Ari yells, "Can I warm up the car?" He was born to make things go. Since he was five years old, he's been sitting on David's lap steering the car for fun. Getting his driver's license at sixteen will be just a formality. I toss him the key and run upstairs to the bedroom.

As I rummage through a box on the dresser for my wedding ring, David mumbles sleepily, "Have a great day, honey," then rolls over on his side. He pulls his old blue blanket over his head, so he looks like an Arab sultan with his head wrap and beard.

We inherited my parents' wedding bands, but hardly ever wear them. I remember my mother's large-boned hands with flat apricot-tinted nails when I slip on the heavy, swirled gold band. At first I wanted to restyle it to make it more graceful, but I couldn't. Couldn't quite carve up Bernice's ring, or lighten the weight of her spirit. The rings sit on the dresser, snug together, oxidizing in the box. The story I'll tell today, "Leah and the Tiger," gave my ring a new purpose.

After I drop off Ari at the middle school, I walk down the hall to the classroom where I'll do a storytelling demonstration for two classes. It's part of an esteem-building program for at-risk kids where I teach sixth graders to tell folktales, then take them to elementary schools to perform.

The teacher announces, "This is Debbie Zaslow," as I enter. "Some of you will be working with her for the next five weeks." Even though many of them know me from storytelling in their elementary schools, they peer skeptically, shifting in their seats as I walk to the front of the classroom.

I explain that storytellers often change folktales to fit them. "This is one I've done radical surgery on," I tell them. "It used to be called, 'Why Women Won't Listen.'" I wait until I hear the mock gasps from girls and groans from boys that always follow the announcement of this title. "My version is called 'Leah and the Tiger.' Listen, and try to figure out what I've changed, then tell me afterward." Curiosity piqued, they're silent as I begin.

Once, long ago, in the islands of the West Indies, there lived a man and his wife who had an only daughter, Leah. She was so lovely that all the young men on the neighboring islands wanted to marry her, and they bothered her night and day.

I watch the audience as I tell. Sixth graders are gawky creatures, having fallen off the top of the pile at the elementary school and landed on new ground. They inch around, feeling out their territory here, terrified at not fitting in. Some of them glance about to see if it's okay to be enthralled with a story, then stare back at me vacantly. Some, determined to be cool, slouch in their seats, appearing not to listen. Many are wide-eyed, already in the story-trance.

In the story Leah's family shuts her away in a jungle hut to keep the suitors away. Her mother brings food every day and sings a song at the doorway to signal her arrival. *Leah, Leah, ting-a-ling ling/ Honey at the door, Darling/ Sugar at the door, ting-a-ling-ling/ Sugar at the door, Darling.* When I sing this refrain with exaggerated sweet innocence, the students fidget and eyeball each other. Is this kids' stuff? Is this okay? Then my voice takes on an ominous edge. *Don't open the door unless you hear MY voice singing this song. DON'T open the door to anyone else.* Now it sounds scary. It must be cool.

A tiger tries to trick Leah into opening the door by imitating the song on her porch. I assume the lecherous stance of the tiger, then boom out in a foolish, gruff voice, "*Leah Leah Ting a Ling Ling/ Honey at the door Darling!*" The kids are cracking up now; this is definitely cool.

In the original story, the tiger goes to the blacksmith, who sticks a poker down his throat to sweeten up his rough voice. The tiger returns to the porch two more times until he sounds just right. When Leah opens the door, he pounces on her and devours her, bones and all. The father blames it on the mother, who failed to bring Leah home when he told her to. The mother dies of fright when he yells at her, and then the father dies of grief. End of story.

Even though the ending didn't seem to fit, I liked the story. I wanted Leah to be transformed at adolescence, though, instead of shamed, frightened, and eaten. The obvious change would be for her emerge from the belly of the tiger, like Red Riding Hood, or Jonah and the Whale. When I adapt a story I visualize the characters and objects and see where they lead. In this story Leah wears a "valuable ring of pearls and gold." I closed my eyes and imagined Leah guiding me into the belly of the tiger where it was dark and airless, suffocatingly silent. The gold and pearl ring glowed like pale moonlight.

The ring could lead Leah out, but how would she get it in the first place? This time I pictured Leah's mother handing her the ring, slipping it onto her finger. "*This ring belonged to my mother, and before that my mother's mother. The ring gets its power from the light of the moon. Wear it in the moonlight and it will protect you.*"

In my version, Leah's mother gives her the ring before they go to the hut and each night as she walks in the moonlight, the ring grows brighter. When the tiger finally tricks her into opening the door, the ring slips off her finger as he pounces on her and then devours her.

As I tell it now to the sixth graders, even the skeptics are rapt. *Leah's mother arrived at the hut and found the door swinging open. Inside there was no trace of Leah, just her gold and pearl ring lying in a pool of blood.* She carries the ring home where it grows more luminous every night as the moon grows fuller until the ring speaks. "*Moonlight shining on the pearl. Take me, take me, to the girl.*" The ring guides Leah's parents through the jungle to the tiger's lair where they wrap it in a piece of meat and wait for the tiger to eat it.

As soon as the ring entered the tiger, it found its way onto Leah's finger and her bones began to reassemble themselves and her body began to flesh itself out. From deep inside the belly of the tiger, she stretched and strained and climbed until her hand, with its shining gold and pearl ring, popped out of the tiger's jaw.

I imitate the tiger, moaning with a stomachache, as I stick my arm straight out until I can see my own mother's gold and pearl ring gleaming. *Leah twisted and kicked and pushed with all her strength until she pulled herself up and out of the belly of the tiger. She stood glowing in the moonlight.* The sixth graders cheer as Leah banishes the tiger from the jungle forever.

Afterward, a pair of twelve year-old girls in bright mini-skirts grin at me as they hum *Leah, Leah, Ting-a-ling-ling* while walking to their next class. Outside in the parking lot, I pause. The fall air in Southern Oregon is crisp, and the field a brilliant moss green, surrounded by the Siskiyou and Cascade Mountains. I finger my mother's ring, solid on my finger, gently rub the pearls, and speak to her. *I know I'm going into the belly of the tiger. Help me to stretch enough to give Bubbe what she needs to pass on. Help me do the right thing.*

As soon as I get home, I go downstairs to check on preparations for Bubbe. If you peeked at the soft foods in the cupboards and fingered the stacks of clean blankets, you'd be sure we were expecting a baby in our newly stocked room. Marilyn called yesterday and agreed to be the main caregiver, so things seem to be falling into place. A friend of hers, Shayla, will take the weekday shifts, and another friend of theirs, Karen, is taking the weekends. None of them has much experience, but they're willing to try and I'm relieved to have a crew lined up.

Last night our dog got out, wandered into the street, was hit by a car and broke his pelvis. Though it was late at night, the kids insisted on going with us to the vet. Rachel sobbed while Ari fought back tears as he helped lift Charlie into the car. They stroked and comforted him as he whimpered all the way there. *Will they be this caring about their Bubbe?*

Charlie hobbles around today, frail, wincing in pain, needing constant attention. He barks and whines at the top of the stairs because he can't climb down to be with me. As I open the door to the stairway to see him peering at me, I'm struck by an image of my mother. I see her at the end of her life, at fifty-two, pale from pancreatic cancer. In the months before her death, my father cared for her at home, measuring doses of pain medicine into syringes, squeezing them into her dimpled flesh. I went home for a month to help my father take care of her, then headed back to college in Oregon. My mother phoned a few days after I left. Each time I heard her voice it was thinner, reedier, fading with her body. She said, "Today I tried to go down the stairs to go out, but I'm not strong enough. I guess I can never go out again."

She sounded like a trapped, frightened child, and I knew it was really the end of her life. I wanted to hear her strong again, gabbing on the phone, dispensing advice, sipping martinis, smoking Lucky Strikes, laughing too loud. Wanted to see her stride up and down those stairs; to stop her body from evaporating with the wisps of her voice. I planned to fly back in two weeks, after finals, for whatever time she had left, but she died two days before I was scheduled to go.

I help Charlie limp down the stairs, one step at a time. Below us the metal rails of Bubbe's new bed gleam. I don't stop to think that maybe I'm bringing Bubbe here because I couldn't be with my mother at her death. I can't really see the hole in my heart or hear my mother's voice. Bubbe's voice is all I hear, as if she's calling from under deep water. I'm answering her, ready or not.

five

David and I leave for L.A. tomorrow morning. The women in our congregation gather this evening for *Rosh Hodesh*, the new moon celebration. Even though I'm frazzled, I want to go because I need to be in the cocoon of women. We wash each other's hands and recite the names of our female ancestors in Hebrew, calling them into our circle. I dip my hands in the warm fluid, let them be dried gently and say, *"I'm Devorah, Bat Bracha, Bat Soiralaya, Bat Shoshana.* Debra, daughter of Bernice, daughter of Lena, daughter of Rose."

Sue, who is hosting the gathering this month, has an auto-immune disease that put her in a wheelchair for the last ten years. She carries herself regally erect, her long dark hair billowing, as she glides to the front of the circle. She translates the story of Judith, who saved her people from Holofernes as he was plotting to kill the Jews. *Judith was a widow and when she was done with her mourning she pulled off her sackcloth, washed and anointed herself, braided her hair, and went to the camp of Holofernes. After several days of flattery and lies, she had him right where she wanted him, alone and passed-out drunk. Judith prayed to God for strength, then grabbed Holofernes' hair with one hand, and with the other she sliced off his head. Then she put it in her bag and left the camp.*

It's quiet for a moment. We're used to violence in Torah stories, but this one is really graphic. Sue breaks the silence. "So, could you do what Judith did?"

A tall woman named Rebecca says, "Even if I had to save a whole people, I couldn't chop a head off," and most of the women nod.

Aja, Sue's seventeen year-old daughter says, "It doesn't do any good to use violence, it only creates more violence. Look at the Middle East."

Dana, who lost her husband five years ago, says, "I can see why it was a widow who did this. When you have nothing to lose, you could do anything."

I offer the metaphoric approach. "Maybe it's not whether we could actually chop a head off, but if we can use Judith's image when we need courage to face something head-on in our lives and slice through it."

I could use some courage right now, so I ask for blessings for what I'm about to undertake. The women gather around me, hands raised. My eyes close and my hands open to receive, as they offer their words.

> *May you keep your balance as you care for your grandmother.*
> *I know it's hard to give up your space. May you return to it renewed.*
> *May you reap the growth in this for you.*
> *Know that if things get really tough you can always come*
> *   to me and scream.*
> *May you keep your sense of humor.*
> *May the love that you put forth be returned to you on many levels.*
> *Amen.*

BEST CASE SCENARIO: We get Bubbe and the plane ride and transfer are smooth. She settles in with peace and serenity because of the intense caring that is offered to her and accepted graciously by her. The children are eager to spend time with her as they gain new appreciation of their wise Bubbe and their hearts stretch to the max. Everyone around her is moved and her presence here is just what her soul needs for these last few months of her life. We grow as a family, and Bubbe finally gets the love and support she never had, so she can pass on peacefully. She does so, gracefully, and within a few months. We bury her with sadness and closure, then rearrange our house to go back to our lives, changed and glowing. When I arrive in Heaven at the end of my long, satisfying life there is a special chair with an inscription that commends me for the Great Mitzvah that I was Called to do. *She overcame her fears and sacrificed for Bubbe. She did the right thing.* In Gold Letters.

WORST CASE SCENARIO: We go to get her but she doesn't want to go. She's confused and angry and combative on the plane ride and forever. She becomes totally incontinent and is up all night. The caregivers quit. The children don't want to go near her because they're disgusted and frightened and besides they want their own lives. I'm tense and angry and ashamed of my feelings, so I alienate everyone in my family. Every time I try to get close to Bubbe to comfort her I feel the confused, jumbly shadow of the anger in my family and I shrink from her. Sensing this, she is miserable. David immerses himself in work and pretends that everything is okay, since it's okay with him, and he's no help or comfort to me. I feel alone, abandoned, guilty, and ashamed. My out-of-town family calls every five minutes and drives me crazy. Bubbe lives forever in misery, completely disrupting our lives. We are never reimbursed for her expenses, which are astronomical. Ari becomes a juvenile delinquent because Bubbe moved in just when he was on the brink of adolescence and I wasn't able to be there for him. Rachel hates me because all of the woman-hatred in our family is stirred up by Bubbe's presence. David leaves because it's no fun at home any more. When I get to Heaven the chair reads, *You Schmuck, you should have listened to those voices in the night.*

PREDICTED REALITY: Somewhere in between.

On the way to the airport the next morning David chatters away as I stare out the window. My neck is so tight that it occurs to me that if we were in a car accident it would snap exactly in two. "What about a tranquilizer for Bubbe tomorrow?" David asks. I tell him that I've already explained to him sixty times that we can give her Atavan an hour before she goes on the plane.

"Not sixty times," he says.

He talks about how exciting this is for him because he wasn't able to be there at the actual moment of his mother's or father's death and he feels guilty. I tell him that the chances of us being there at the exact moment of Bubbe's death are slim, since we've arranged round-the-clock caregivers so that we can continue to lead our lives.

David goes on for a while about how you know someone is dying, how when they enter a final state called *Gosech*, their breathing changes and their eyes turn inward. I endure this, resisting the urge to tell him that I am quite aware of this from having worked in nursing homes and hospitals when I was in college. I wish he'd shut up.

He keeps talking about how wonderful it will be, how something of special value will come out of it for me, a healing, a new attitude, perhaps something intangible, subtle.

Don't you think I have already thought of this? I don't say it.

He says, "It won't be as hard as you think, Deb, because we have help."

"David, she's going to need *me* at first—do you think I'm going to take her away from her familiar surroundings and leave her with strangers and visit her only once a day? I'm going to be there a lot!"

"But eventually," he says, "she'll settle in."

"Eventually," I say, "she'll die."

On the plane to Los Angeles, David sits on the aisle, with me in the middle. A little old woman with white hair hobbles down the aisle, then squeezes past us into the window seat. I mentally dub her "The Practice Grandma." I try to ignore her as I fiddle with things and stare straight ahead.

"I'm going to visit my daughter," she says softly. I nod, and smile half-heartedly. "My husband died this year. Sixty-two years we were married and now I'm alone." I surrender, turn toward her and listen. She goes on for a while, just needing to talk. I nod, smile, nod. David dozes happily. When the Practice Grandma stops talking, I lean on David's shoulder and feel sucked into sleep, like anesthesia before a surgery.

In the motel that night I dream that Bubbe and I float in a swimming pool. She reaches under my arms to lift me, but I think, "No, I should lift her," so I reach for her. We lift each other and float together in the water. I can't really hear her words, but we understand each other perfectly.

The next morning at the nursing home David and I walk down the hall to Bubbe's room. Everything is strewn about: piles of clothes, old photos, garbage bags bulging, suitcases half filled. The room bustles with people. Aunt Minnie stands out, plump, white-haired, eighty-five years old and dressed in a red and black stretchy outfit topped with a velvet beret, tipped at a rakish angle. My cousin Tom, and his wife, Tracy, are here, along with Bubbe's personal attendant, and the nursing home owner and her son, who wears a yellow knit yarmulke. Everyone mills about. There's an odd circus-like atmosphere with Bubbe sitting right in the middle.

"Nobody esked me!" she hisses. Her eyes peer from their deep sockets, hard like dark marbles, accusing. Her hands tug at her skirt, then flail at nothing. "Nobody esked me! Nobody esked me!"

Tracy, a big blond woman who converted to Judaism twenty-five years ago to marry Tom, strokes Bubbe's hand and speaks slowly, as if to a child. "We asked you . . . Bubbe . . . but . . . you don't . . . remember." This is a lie. Minnie mentioned it to Bubbe a few days ago, after it was already decided, the wheels in motion, like a runaway train.

I sit down and take Bubbe's hand. "The *children* want you, Bubbe, Rachel and Ari want to have their Bubbe near them." This, of course, is a big lie, but it seems to work. She stops shouting and flailing and spits loudly into a tissue.

"She spits all the time now," Minnie says. This, I see, is true. Large, loud, phlegm-filled gobs at a rate of about one every thirty seconds. Minnie explains, "If you scream at her, 'DON'T DO THAT!' then she stops." She demonstrates this technique loudly for me, but I motion to her to stop.

"Thanks, Minnie, it's okay." I make a mental note to buy a few hundred boxes of Kleenex.

Finally we roll Bubbe down the hall. She is dressed in a sweet, pink cotton jumper with a huge diaper underneath. I know I won't be able to take her to the bathroom on the airplanes, so I insisted on the diaper. She had her hair "done" at the retirement home salon this morning into a helmet of tight curls that doesn't quite go with her ancient face. This hairdo looks like it isn't going anywhere, while her face is clearly making its way back to the earth.

Everyone from the room trails out after us to say goodbye. David and Tom lift Bubbe into the backseat of the car, as she howls in protest. David wrenches his back. Minnie says goodbye to her mother, knowing this is probably the last time she'll ever see her. I was expecting a tear or two, but she seems calm and sort of cavalier. The red beret helps.

We transfer Bubbe from the car to the wheelchair again at the Burbank Airport, and proceed to the counter. She is now wearing her blue wool coat with a fox fur collar, saved from some indefinable era. She looks lost in it, her face sinking down to the fur, her dark eyes darting about anxiously. I had hoped the tranquilizer would have kicked in by now, but I see it is no match for Bubbe. She's alert. She's awake. She's planning to be present.

The flight is delayed, so we get Bubbe a muffin, which I feed her bit by bit as she gums it down. We follow up this success with some frozen yogurt, but she spits it out loudly. We sit. We wait. People pass by with their briefcases and smile at old Bubbe in her wheelchair. I consider offering her to the strangers. "Excuse me, I've made a terrible mistake. Would you like the opportunity to do a *mitzvah?*"

When it's finally time to board, David wheels Bubbe outside to meet the special attendants behind the airplane. They lift her out of her wheelchair into a crane-like apparatus. Her eyes are huge, her jaw rigid, but she's helpless against these strong men. One of the employees rides up with her to the top of the air-stairs, where David and I then inch her down the airplane aisle with her walker. We each hold one shoulder from behind as Bubbe totters along, bewildered.

We seat her between us in the first bulkhead aisle. Her face is frozen as she stares ahead, her hands gripping the seat handles. When we're airborne, I stroke her hand and talk to her soothingly. David, on the other side, reads a prayer book and acts as if he were on any old flight. I lean over Bubbe and whisper loudly to him, " I want you to be *present,* be here with me, with Bubbe."

He replies calmly, "I'm doing what I need to do. Prayer is important."

"Help me out!" My voice is rising over the airplane din. "Be doting to Bubbe. She needs it. I need you!"

"She's doing fine, Debbie. Just try to relax!"

Bubbe, who doesn't miss a trick even when she's hurtling through the air to an unknown destination, peers up at us while we argue at a volume she can't possibly hear. "Is he med?" she asks me.

"No," I lie.

"Does he get med a lot?" She gives me a knowing look, lips pursed, one eyebrow tilted. I remember my grandpa Morris was a sour, angry man and they bickered constantly.

"No," I say, and this time it is the truth. David is not that kind of man.

I sit in a straight-backed wooden chair in my grandmother's kitchen. At nine years old I'm spending the weekend because my parents are out of town and Grandma is making me scrambled-eggs-flopsy for breakfast. She turns on the stove by flicking the dial until the blue flame bursts out. Her hair is in tight, gray curls. She "vashes her head" only once a week and doesn't dye it or have it done like my friend Laurie's grandma, who is modern. She wears an old flowered housecoat with faded slippers that bulge out from her bunions.

She drops a fat slab of butter into the little iron skillet, where it melts and sizzles as she scrambles up the eggs, then throws them into the pan to swim in the butter. She slides them onto the plate while they are still very loose. It's the only food that my grandma cooks that I like.

When the back door opens, Grandma rolls her eyes, heavenward. "Here comes my old man," she announces. The stale smoky smell of Grandpa's cigar wafts into the kitchen before he does. Grandma says he used to be handsome, but to me he just looks kind of crumpled and sour.

"Vere's my coffee?" Grandpa sits down without looking at either of us.

"Vere's his coffee? He vants to know vere's his coffee. Vere does he tink?" She directs this at me, but I look blank.

"She tinks I kent hear." My grandpa continues the conversation with me as the unwilling target. I know I don't have to say anything, but it makes me squirm in my chair.

Grandma gets up, pours some coffee into a saucepan, and turns on the stove full blast. "He hess to hev it boiling hot," she says to me. "So, vat am I gonna do? I boil it for him."

"Should I drink it cold?" Grandpa stares at me. "She vants me to drink it cold."

"Like I don't boil it for him every day." She doesn't bother looking at me this time, just sets it front of him, hard. He picks it up and gulps it down. "His stomach is like steel," she says. "Someday it vill kill him."

"She'd like to see dat day, if she lives dat long. *Zie gezundt.*" Grandpa gets up from the table and slams the back door as he goes outside.

He will go back in the garage and eventually he'll live to be ninety-two. His last years will be spent in a nursing home where she will hardly ever come to see him because she doesn't drive and he won't remember her anyway. She will live to be one hundred-and-three and come spend her last days in my house, but nobody knows this sitting in the kitchen in 1960. I look up to see a sign above the sink. It's a carved, painted, wooden rooster who appears to be sweating. The caption under it, in red letters, reads, "The First Hundred Years Are the Hardest."

⌒〜

When we finally pull into our driveway with Bubbe at eleven o'clock at night, Shayla and Marilyn, the main caregivers, stand at the door, with Rachel and Ari right behind them. We sit Bubbe on her new bed and she blinks, her eyes flitting around the room. She smiles at the kids and pats their heads. Rachel and Ari say goodnight and David goes upstairs with them to put an icepack on his back.

Marilyn and I awkwardly change Bubbe into some nightclothes. When I breathe the stench from her diaper I wonder if this smell will be permeating our household for a while. We do as little wiping as possible—getting her right to sleep is the priority. She lies down, glances around, closes her eyes, and begins to snore in minutes. I let out the first long breath I have breathed all day, and go upstairs to bed.

About one a.m. I wake to hear footsteps on the stairs. Marilyn needs my help. I grab my robe and stumble downstairs, where Bubbe is sitting up in bed, glaring. Her hands flail, clenching and unclenching as if getting ready for a punch. "Vy did dey take me to Debbie's? Vy didn't any vun esk me?" she repeats over and over again. No answer satisfies her.

Finally, Marilyn, in a stroke of bona fide genius, says firmly, "WELL BUBBE, IT'S VERY LATE. WHY DON'T WE GO TO SLEEP NOW AND WE'LL ASK YOU IN THE MORNING?" Bubbe fixes her eyes on Marilyn, who nods at her calmly. Her hands stop flailing in midair and drift down to her lap. Marilyn tucks the covers around her as she settles into her pillow, and closes her eyes.

Dim lights, hushed voices, a sick room, a crisis. I am limp, washed of all feeling. My sleep is tense, fitful, as I wake to listen for what's going on downstairs. The new baby has arrived.

PART II

Tornado Touches Down

A long anticipated visit from a powerful being.
Closing one finger at a time, he has struck the land with his gray fist
Shattering, disregarding the laws of man.
–Earth Voices Deck, Robert Beridha

six

November 20, 1996

Inside my dream I hear voices rising from under the floorboards. I force myself awake and head downstairs where Bubbe sits up in bed, her eyes darting around, as if searching for enemy fire.

She zeroes in on me as I walk over, take her hand, and kiss her cheek. "How are you this morning, Bubbe?" I ask.

She grips my hand, then sighs as she leans her head back on the pillow. "Vell, I'm here," she says.

"Me, too."

Shayla has taken Marilyn's place and together we clean Bubbe, dress her, and change the sheets. This takes nearly two hours and exhausts all three of us. Her bones seem gargantuan, fairly clanking under her thin, papery skin. She doesn't want to be washed or shuffled around and she grows heavier with every move. Her mouth is pinched tight and her eyes track me around the room, making me feel vaguely guilty, as if I've committed a secret crime.

As we dress her, I look at her long, slack breasts and the wide hipbones jutting out below her rib cage. I remember my seventh-grade homemaking teacher measuring me for the A-line shift I was struggling with in sewing class. Tape encircling me, pins in mouth, she declared, "You have high hips." I was as ashamed as if she had announced it over the school P.A. system.

Now, years later, I face the source of those hips. My grandmother, while her flesh crumbles toward the earth, still carries a pelvis wide and strong enough to spring forth generations of powerful, but unfashionably high, hips.

Once we have Bubbe out of bed and washed, we decide to try a first trip outside in the wheelchair. Again I'm reminded of the first weeks with a baby, when each outing is filled with special, new equipment and layers of clothing. Bubbe can hold her head up better than a new baby, but her feet are another matter. Swollen stiff and stuffed into red fuzzy slippers, they slide off the wheelchair footrests, seeming to operate independently of the rest of her. We wedge the feet with towels, then wheel her outside.

Bubbe scowls at the scenery, her eyes bulging every time we roll over a bump. I take a breath of the sharp, clear air, and savor it. "Look at the mountains, see the beautiful trees!" I shout to her.

She nods grimly as her eyes fix on me, narrowing into hard slits. "Vere's your jecket?"

"I'm not cold, Bubbe."

She repeats, like a mantra, "Put on your jecket, you'll get sick! Put on your jecket, you'll get sick!" until I duck behind the wheelchair so she can't see me.

I feel the quick, familiar heat of resentment rising in my chest, and I'm instantly ashamed. She's a weak, feeble old lady. How could anyone resent her? I brought her here to offer her love and comfort, but despite the good intentions, we both hold on to our personalities, the patterns playing like grooves in a worn record.

Once we settle her back into her room, Shayla fixes Bubbe's lunch while I run upstairs to eat alone. When I come back down, she looks at her food, then at me, and squints. "You're not eating anyting!" Another flash from the pit of my stomach—how I hated it when she said that while I was growing up! I tell her as firmly as I can, "I already ate, Bubbe." This time she doesn't pursue it. She's as tired as I am. She likes her food, though, and eats a lot of macaroni and cheese, gumming it loudly, tapping her spoon.

When she's eating, she has a focus. Otherwise, her hands tap at nothing, wave in the air. I stroke her hand and marvel at her stiff, bulbous fingers, like enormous feelers. We pull out her photo albums, and lean shoulder-to-shoulder as we gaze at the old photographs. Her hands travel over surfaces of the faces as if she's sensing their beings, calling them forth. She peers at her wedding picture, sees herself standing stiff and formal at seventeen, then slowly names the entire poker-faced wedding party. She hesitates at two young women at the end. "Dora Tankenoff and Sarah Pill," she pronounces carefully with a look of faint surprise, as if they showed up today to visit. "Dese ver my chums."

We look at a photo of her with her husband and children, posing ramrod straight, pale as ghosts. "Dat's my old man, Morris . . . dat's me." She gives me a wry smile. Then she names her children: "Dere's Sol, Minnie, Merwin, Derril. . ." She stops for a minute, fingers the face of my mother, Bernice, and says, "Dat's Debbie."

"What about Bernice?" I point to the picture of my mother at about four years old. She wrinkles her brow, glancing back and forth between me and the photo.

She begins again, as if to straighten out the memory, taking it from the top, "Minnie, Sol, Merwin, Derril . . . Debbie." Apparently that's final. I feel a little shaken, as if my mother has reached her hand out from the photo, or the grave, and I am simply here doing something for Bubbe that she could not do.

When I was a child, my grandma would tell me that my mother was a real dickens. "Oy, honey. . .Vat Bernice didn't do. She'd trow her shoes down the toilet, and pull de chain. Vunce she flushed down my mudder's pearl necklace!" Grandma would roll her eyes in mock horror. As a teen, Bernice wore trousers and romped around the city with her cousin Sherman, taking the streetcar wherever it led them. She bossed around her younger sister Derril, who worshipped her. When Derril would trail home from school behind her, Bernice would turn and ask, "Who are you, little girl?"

"I'm Derril! Don't you remember me?" Derril would wail, but Bernice's coolness to her sister's pleas was legendary.

Aunt Derril recently sent me a faded news clipping of my mother as a teenager with a girls' club called the "Trampers." They're posed outdoors, dressed in dungarees and halter tops, hairdos curled but windblown. I ask my friends now if they can guess which one is my mother. They hesitate; this is a blurry Xerox of an old news photo, and all the girls look similar. "Which one seems the most alive?" I prompt, and they invariably point to my mother, beautiful and glowing in the center, the others revolving around her like a wheel.

My favorite photo of my mother is her graduation picture, at seventeen. She stands in a white dress, holding a bouquet of flowers. Her face is olive-skinned and broad, her dark eyes serious. She stands next to a tree that is as solid and rooted as her large-boned frame. She holds the flowers away from her body, as if she were about to throw them off at any moment and hoist herself into the tree to pose, wild-eyed and confident.

My fingers graze over the photo, stroking her face. I want to turn her towards the tree. *Press your face to the trunk, smell the resin. Listen, you can hear beetles climbing in rows, racing through the core of the wood.* I want her to grab the trunk and hold it so fiercely that her life doesn't drain away. I want to shout, *Hold on and don't move. Everything you need is here.* But she can't hear me. She smoothes her gown and stares ahead.

By late afternoon Bubbe and I are both worn out. After we put away the photo albums, Shayla and I settle her into bed, where she starts to snore in seconds.

In the evening she grows restless, coughing, spitting loudly, refusing her medicines and pushing Shayla away. When I come downstairs she calms a little, so I stay as long as I can, talking softly, holding her hand. When we finally dim the lights in her room I go upstairs, but I sleep lightly, unable to tune out noises below me, sensing her unrest.

First thing in the morning I head downstairs, where Shayla meets me at the door, pale and wide-eyed. "I quit," she says.

"What happened?" I can see that Bubbe is still in bed, awake but drowsy, glancing around, then closing her eyes.

"She was up all night." Shayla's voice is high pitched, frightened. "I couldn't understand what she wanted. She kept saying something like 'Hame, Hame!' When I tried to comfort her, she waved her hands and pushed me away."

I explain that Bubbe was probably saying the Yiddish word *Haim*, meaning home, because she's confused about where she is. Shayla tells me that *she* was confused and nervous all night, and ended up sitting in the bathroom, because she didn't want to be pushed away. I hired Shayla knowing she was emotionally fragile, but I thought her innate kindness was what we most needed. Apparently not. I swallow down a bubble of panic. I've taken a week off at the middle school, but how will I find time to hire another caregiver so I can go back to work?

Bubbe's new doctor comes, which takes an hour of examining and talking. The hospice nurse, Diane, makes her first visit. Another hour of talking and examining and talking. Shouting, actually, since Bubbe can't hear anything unless it is at the volume of a megaphone, and I'm her interpreter. She's cordial to all the visitors. "Haw nice to meet you." She smiles at the hospice nurse and stares at her bright red suit and high-heeled pumps. "Det's a nice outfit," she says as she reaches out and fingers the fabric.

The caregivers aren't sure how to care for Bubbe, so I help them walk her to the bathroom, dab at her bottom, fuss with her sheets, try new foods, and shuffle to the bathroom again. After one trip she reaches to wipe herself, then smears feces all over the bathroom walls, sink, and anywhere she can reach. As we clean her up, I wipe her bottom as gently as I can. She turns and howls at me, "YOU'RE KILLING ME! YOU'RE KILLING ME!"

In the afternoon Bubbe and I sit on the old green sofa by the window, lean into each other and slow our breath. She glimpses around, every now and then naming something, as if orienting herself. "Tree," she says and I repeat it and nod, "Tree." A few minutes later she says, "Chair," and I confirm it. She stares at the leaves outside and says, "Dis is like a park here."

I lean closer and ask, "Bubbe, do you think you want to stay here?"

She knits her brow, as if studying a chess move. "Do you vant me here?"

"Yes." I nod. She sinks into me, so I feel her hoarse breathing, her soft cheek against mine.

"Does David vant me?" As if on cue, he enters from the back door.

"Here he is. Why don't you ask him?"

Bubbe looks up at him. "Do you mind me hangin' on your vife like dis?"

David takes in the scene, then kneels and grasps Bubbe's hand. "I don't mind at all."

seven

Each morning I descend the stairs to Bubbe's room and come up for air at bedtime. It's lucky if I can sneak upstairs for a shower, and if I find time to go out, I'm too exhausted to speak to anyone. Apparently I've forgotten how to say anything interesting anyway, so it's better that I keep my mouth shut. Again, this is very much like new motherhood, but the baby is not as cute, much harder to lift, and she spits like a sailor.

The hands-on work with Bubbe would be plenty, but I'm also searching for another caregiver, shopping for special food, keeping track of medications, and explaining everything to everybody about a hundred times, including members of my extended family who call at all hours.

Relative: How is everything going with Bubbe?

Me: Well, she seems to be settling in.

Bubbe in the background: Dis vater is terrible! (She spits loudly.)

Me (to caregiver): When she asks for water, just give her juice.

Relative: Is there something wrong with the water? Is Bubbe choking?

Caregiver: Here's some nice water. Now drink this, Bubbe.

Me (wiping spit off myself): No, everything is fine.

Relative: You know you have to be careful when you hire caregivers. One of them accidentally almost killed my friend's mother by giving her the wrong medicines. Make sure you look at the labels on all the bottles and...

Caregiver: Here, Bubbe, you can swallow this pill. Just take a sip of water.
Bubbe: Vat's dis for?
Relative: You really should monitor everything that goes into Bubbe.
Me: You're right. I've got to go.
Relative: You are such a saint to take your grandmother in. I don't know how you do it.
Me (dodging a tissue full of prune juice and spit flying through the air): Me neither.

My immediate family goes on as if nothing much has happened, which it hasn't, actually, to them. The kids go to school and David goes to work while I go downstairs to another world. David says, "You're doing too much. Just let the caregivers take over." This, he explains, is what he did when his father was dying in Florida. "The caregivers did the physical work, and I visited with my father." He says this as if it were the most logical thing in the world. Never mind that his father was in his own home and the caregivers were professionals.

"I didn't bring her all the way here to leave her in confusion while she's getting adjusted," I wail at David.

When he spends time with Bubbe, he plays guitar as she claps along with him, or he puts on his prayer shawl and holds her hand while they pray. These moments, though, are rare. When he told me he'd spend an hour a day with her, I should have known it wasn't realistic because he's so busy, but I *wanted* it to be true. I let the mental picture of him sitting with Bubbe in the nursing home, stroking her hand, be the catalyst to bring her here, the image that I held onto.

The reality is starkly different. When I close my eyes I picture a kind of slow-motion rewind where Bubbe fades out and my life falls neatly back into order. But she is there when I wake in the morning, all day, and all night. Escaping to be by myself is impossible, since my office is full of David and his furniture—more foreign objects in this new, crowded life.

At the end of the third day I fall into bed sobbing. David reaches over to me. I'm so frustrated with him that I want to pull away, but I crave the comfort of his touch. As he begins to rub my shoulders I let a little of the tension melt into his hand.

My romance with David started in 1978 when I was a student teacher in a second grade class. In those days I wore snug sweaters, A-line skirts, and mid-calf boots. A little older and wiser than the other student teachers, I'd been in and out of college for ten years, changing majors, smoking pot, going through a divorce from an early marriage, and watching my mother die. My life was finally shaping up: no more nonsense, drugs, or unreliable men. On a Thursday afternoon at one-fifteen P.M., after recess, as my students filed back into the classroom, we looked at the board to see what was next. It read, "*1:15 –1:45 David Zaslow, Poet.*"

Fifteen minutes later when the visiting poet had not appeared, the kids were restless, scrambling out of their seats, running to the window. They loved visits from *David Zaslow, Poet,* and had been excited all morning. I glanced down at my schedule for the day and began composing a stinging speech in my mind. If he showed up, I would inform him that his disregard for our time schedule would make us late for gym class and we would, therefore, have to cancel. I would lead him firmly out the door.

The door opened and the children squealed as David entered. He was tall and lank with a mass of dark curly hair, and long, 1970's sideburns. He wore faded corduroys with a denim shirt and a tie slung casually around his neck, like an afterthought. He was grinning so wildly that his eyes were sparkly slits. My students leapt from their seats, surrounding him, bouncing, giggling, tugging at his shirt, and reaching to strum his guitar. He crouched down to greet them, then glanced up at me.

His eyes widened. "*You're* the student teacher here?" He stood slowly as he took my hands in his. I knew he'd seen me at the jazz club that he owned in Ashland. I nodded dumbly.

"You're fifteen minutes late," I said, halfheartedly.

"I am so sorry." He gazed into my eyes. "We were writing such amazing poems in Mrs. Cady's class that we lost track of time. I hope it's not a problem. Do we still have some time here?"

The kids hollered, "Yes!"

"Of course." I grinned back at him.

David swung his guitar around and began strumming, then adlibbing a refrain as he invited kids to fill in their own words. When he sang their words back, he pronounced them with reverence, as if hearing each word for the first time. The children glowed as they sang along. David led them to call out metaphors and weave them into group poems. "The moon is a cheeseburger! The clouds are French fries!" They finished by writing their own poems, gripping their stubby pencils, eyes on fire.

My class was fifteen minutes late to gym class. David and I were married two and a half years later.

David keeps rubbing my shoulders as my sobbing subsides. He whispers, "You're doing such an important thing, Devorah. Much bigger than you know. You're being called. Something in your soul is doing something for Bubbe's soul. I know it has to do with you and Rachel and your mother." I wish I could hear the call, but I'm too busy with Bubbe's body to hear anything else. The body is so frail, though, that I sense the soul just below the surface of her withered skin, as if you could just scrape gently and underneath would be a tender secret.

eight

The phone wakes me at seven a.m. when the hospice administrator calls. *Do you think that the generic brand of the stool softener will do? Which company manufactures the morphine cream? Do you need one or two part-time caregivers?* As I stumble with the phone into the kitchen I find myself in a heap of paperwork before I'm fully awake.

Rachel walks in, rubbing her eyes, her ponytail sticking straight up on top of her head. "What are *you* doing up?" she asks.

"I'm trying to straighten things out. The doctor wants Bubbe to have certain medicines but hospice has to approve them, and I'm still trying to find another caregiver." I want to keep explaining, eager to have someone, anyone, to tell it to, but Rachel has already lost interest.

She peers into the refrigerator. "Don't we have any eggs?" Her eyes are wide, incredulous. Valley Girl meets a third world country. "I put them on the list *two days* ago. Does anyone ever go shopping around here anymore?"

Normally I'd make a snappy retort. "Forgive me, oh Princess, I forgot, your wish is my command," or, "Are you allergic to Cornflakes?" Instead I burst into tears.

"Mom, all I asked is why don't we have eggs? What did I *do?*" Rachel glances around as if looking for someone else to replace this new, exasperating mother.

"I'm just overwhelmed. I don't have time to go to the store, I don't have time to take a shower, I don't have time for anything, and nobody's exactly helping me out!"

"Well, don't look at me. I've got tons of homework. I'm in high school now, Mom, remember? *High school?* I have rehearsals every day. Are you even going to have time to come to my play?"

"Of course I'm coming. I just didn't know it would be so crazy with Bubbe here." I lay my head on the pile of papers on the table. "At least I thought I'd still get sleep."

Rachel walks over and sits next to me. I see through the crook in my elbow her bright blue pajama bottoms, feel her warmth. I expect her to say something comforting, but instead she gazes at me with cool, dark eyes and says, "I told you so."

I stare back, blinking.

She gets up, strides over to the cupboard and pulls out a box of cereal. "Want some?"

I shake my head and force a smile. "I hate Cornflakes, don't we have any eggs?"

My family's nonchalance over Bubbe surprises me, Rachel's most of all. She doesn't want to spend time with her, as if that would be giving in to my bad idea, and make it easier on me. *Don't look at me. I told you so.* On Sunday, when she wanted a ride to the local nursing home, I asked, "Why don't you and Kate stay here and spend a few hours with Bubbe instead?"

She shot back, "I'm not going to abandon all my friends at the nursing home that I've visited for years, just because you decide to bring your grandma home. I hardly know Bubbe."

"But you like old people so much, I thought you'd want to get to know her better."

"I enjoy them at Linda Vista. I don't bring them home."

Well, apparently, I *do* bring them home, and nobody around here is cutting me any slack. *One day at a time,* I tell myself, *everyone's reactions are normal. We'll all adjust eventually.* But I'm not sure I believe it.

I can't help thinking the timing is a little off. A few years ago both kids would have been more eager to be around Bubbe. Six years ago, when Rachel was eight, at a family gathering, she helped Bubbe in and out of her chair, gently offering her arm whenever she got up to walk. In a photo from that weekend Rachel looks intent, her face reaching the height of Bubbe's bosom, as she steers her carefully down a walkway.

Three years ago, at Bubbe's hundredth birthday, Ari hugged her so warmly that she lost her footing. Luckily she was standing in front of her couch, where they both landed, unharmed. On that same visit, when I got frustrated in a conversation with Bubbe, nine-year-old Ari chastised me. "Mom," he mouthed to me, "You're talking too loud. Don't be mean to her."

When Ari's in her room now, he keeps his distance, always eyeing the door. Since that hug three years ago, she's withered into a different being. She's given up wearing dentures, so her cheeks are sunken, her jaw juts, and the few lower front teeth she has are a rotting, soft brown. Her dark lidded eyes seem to follow you from across the room, and when she leans over and motions for Ari to come closer, his eyes bulge. Mostly, he avoids going downstairs. He likes to skateboard in the driveway, though, and if Bubbe is situated so she can see him, he waves to her from a safe distance. "Look at det blondie!" she says to no one in particular as she waves back.

I'd like to skate off into the distance, but when I'm with Bubbe, she takes my hands, then leans her forehead into mine. David calls this position "mind-meld." Her face is so close it's a blur, but I can feel her fuzzy skin and smell her warm breath as she kisses me with loud, slurpy sucks. No matter how much I want to shut her out, she calls me to be more.

In the middle of Bubbe's first week I squeeze in a trip to Shop 'N Kart to load up on diapers, prune juice, latex gloves, and thermometers. I imagine people's lives pretty much line up with their shopping cart items. Mothers push around gallons of milk and economy jars of peanut butter, while college students stock up on frozen dinners, beer, and cigarettes. I tromp through the aisles, pushing two shopping carts (to keep Bubbe's account separate), muttering to myself as I try to decipher both lists. A glance in one cart and you'd peg me for a new mother, which goes with my sloppy clothes and red-rimmed eyes. But what baby drinks prune juice and wears queen-size diapers?

I spot an old friend, Suzy, a single mother with six kids, steering past the naval oranges. Never mind *her* shopping cart. She manages her home and children with a calm I've never managed with just two children and a husband who helps. She attributes this to an unflagging faith in God, another thing I can't always muster or maintain. I tell her what I'm doing with Bubbe. Actually, anyone I run into gets filled in on the details of my current life, since I don't seem to have any boundaries anymore.

Store clerk: Oh I see you have two shopping carts today.

Me: Yes, one is for my one hundred and three-year-old grandmother who needs all kinds of special things and...

Store Clerk: Will that be paper or plastic?

Postman (in front of my house): There's a van blocking your mailbox.

Me: Yes, that's the hospital equipment van. You see, my very old and dying grandmother is staying with us and we have to have a potty chair and special hand rails and...

Postman: Tell them to move the van if you want mail.

I say to Suzy in the produce aisle, "I hope I'm doing the right thing."

She picks up a bag of bright Clementine oranges and drops them into her cart. "I know you are," she says.

The next morning after the kids have gone to school, I snuggle down under the covers, feeling David inching his way over. "Is this my wife? In bed, no phone calls, no running downstairs, my wife, lolling about?"

"Don't get used to it. I don't see much lolling in my immediate future."

"Well, let's enjoy it while we can." David cuddles up, stroking my back.

The answering machine next to the bed snaps on. "Hi, Debbie and David, this is George Campbell. We need to talk about Ari and Jonah. Please call back as soon as you can." I sigh and sit up in bed.

Until this year Ari was a model kid— attentive in school, athletic, and most of all, content. Now that he's in sixth grade he talks on the phone all the time, races around on his skateboard instead of doing his homework, and hangs around with kids who get into trouble.

"Well, I hate to tell you this," George says, when I call back, "but Ari and Jonah were smoking cigarettes on the railroad tracks by the middle school yesterday."

I let out a groan. "I guess I'm not surprised, are you?" David motions to me, curious. I pantomime taking a drag of a cigarette, and he groans, too.

"No, I'm not surprised," George answers. Lately we commiserate with the Campbells a lot. Our strategy is to try to listen, reason with the kids, and temper our emotions. We're liberal, ex-hippie parents who want our children to be safe, yet we're baffled by discipline.

"We'll talk to him after school." David puts his arm around my shoulder. "It'll be alright."

I want to believe this, but in my mind I see Ari smoking cigarettes, cutting school, going straight down those railroad tracks to alcohol, drugs, a long way off where we can't reach him. This is the "all or nothing" syndrome, a thinking pattern common to children of alcoholics. My mom was an alcoholic, her brother was an alcoholic, my sister Nancy's son had a drug problem. It seems inevitable, like quicksand.

When Ari comes home, David and I sit him down. What's going on?" Ari asks.

"George called and told us that you and Jonah were smoking." David lays it out.

Ari puffs out his lower lip, then blows a stream of air straight up. His hair flaps up, off of his eyes for an instant. He glances around to see if there is any way out, then looks back at us. "Yeah. So?"

"So, we're upset to hear that," I say.

"Mom, I'm not a little kid anymore. We were just trying it. Everybody does."

David shoots me a look. *Stay calm.* "Well, I know it's normal to try it," he says, "but we don't want you doing that to yourself. If you want to be a good soccer player, you need good lungs."

"I know that. Can I go meet my friends now? Would you stop making such a big deal?"

I want to burst into tears, but I say quietly, "You can go in a minute. But it *is* a big deal to us; we care about your health. You won't be allowed to go out with your friends all the time if you can't handle the freedom."

"I know. I know. I can handle it!" Ari jumps out of the chair. He's heard this before. We're all beginning to understand that he can do what he wants at this age, and we're pretty powerless. After he races out the door, we sit for a minute shaking our heads.

"He'll be okay. He's a great kid," David says as he heads back downstairs to work. I wish I could drop it and scurry off, but I can't push the sinking sensation out of my chest.

This is bad timing. How am I going to give my kids the attention they need with Bubbe here? My friend Linda says on the phone, "It's a good thing. See it as an opportunity to deal with the stressful stuff in your life, and learn how to detach and handle it differently."

My friend Juli, who is as realistic as I am, says, "This is really bad timing."

On Thanksgiving we have just four friends over for a potluck. We eat our turkey, then troop downstairs to visit Bubbe. Marilyn has cooked turkey and mashed potatoes for Bubbe, who sits up in her chair stirring the potatoes with her spoon, dipping her fingers in with her other hand and licking off the goo.

"Happy Thanksgiving, Bubbe!" Rachel hollers.

"Tenk you very much." Bubbe glances from her potatoes to the visitors and back again. Sandy has tucked a flowery dishtowel as a bib over Bubbe's bright green polyester shirt. Her creased, dusky face looks absurd popping out of the field of color, as if she had poked her head through a cardboard scene for a carnival photo.

She tugs at the bib. "I didn't vant to get potatoes on dis nice blouse." She laughs as though this were very funny, so we all laugh along. Our friends are lined up to meet Bubbe, curious, but stiff. I've begun to notice how people react to old age. To those who are edgy around it, Bubbe is a challenge: shriveled, with features that are exaggerated, large, and loose. When she stares out from under the flaps of her eyelids, she seems to peer straight though you, sensing everything.

One friend hunkers down next to Bubbe and asks, "How are you, Mrs. Kanter?" Bubbe just stares at her and nods. I motion to my friend to talk louder.

"HOW ARE YOU LIKING IT HERE?" You could hear this next door.

"Not too bad. De potatoes are pretty good." We laugh, as if she were jokingly rating a restaurant. When you think about it though, at this stage of her life there's not much to do or see or hear, so taste is important. Whether she's happy or not could depend a lot on the potatoes.

We sit down to watch a video of Bubbe's one-hundredth birthday. We pull her chair close to the television so she can see the faces, then turn up the volume. "Dat's Tommy!" she says, surprised. She glances around, to see if maybe he is here, then looks back again. "Dere's Derril and Norm . . . on TV! Vat are dey talking about?"

Rachel kneels close. "It's a videotape, Bubbe, of your hundredth birthday party. Everyone was wishing you happy birthday!"

"Dat vas my birtday? Ven vas dat?" Bubbe flaps her mouth open, then shakes her head.

"Three years ago. Now you're a hundred and three."

"Not me." Bubbe looks around to see everyone nodding their heads. She furrows her brow, glances from one to the other, then shrugs.

"Look, Bubbe," says Marilyn. "There's Debbie!" She points to the TV. I watch myself stand next to Bubbe three years ago, holding up the poem I wrote for her birthday. I see my hand quiver as I read.

Lena. . . You have given me a link to the past
A sense of your pain that has filtered down through bodies and hearts.
What can I give you?
I offer you this
I am a woman with choices and freedoms
Who has held your pain and wrestled it
A branch still blossoming with roots held firmly in place. . .

I watch my face next to Bubbe's in the video, then look back at her in the room as she glances between then and now, shaking her head in confusion. *I am a woman who has held your pain and wrestled with it.* I've seen traces of her pain in my mother's face, felt it slip in and out of my own heart, like a long, toxic fiber, shaped and reshaped, twisted into different forms. Is that what we're doing here, trying to make sense of it all? I wrestle with her pain now as I fumble to adjust her medications, to make her comfortable in my home. Am I trying to pull and stretch that fiber, see whose pain is whose?

I look like I know what I'm talking about as I read the poem. . . *I offer you this/I am a woman with choices and freedom/a branch still blossoming with roots held firmly in place. . ..* I didn't know that three years later I'd walk out of the video into the last scenes of her life, and now we're scratching out an end to that poem together.

When Marilyn turns off the TV, Bubbe blinks, adjusting her focus to the visitors in the room. "Oy, honey," she says to me. "It's all like a dream."

nine

Nearly a week after Shayla's departure, Sandy, recommended by hospice, arrives with her blond hair in a tidy bun, and a list of neatly typed recommendations in hand. She insists on starting a written log of Bubbe's activities, meals and medications. *Tuesday 8:00 A.M. Sandy Johnson on duty. Marilyn has breakfast ready. Cream of rice made, banana slices in a bowl and a can of fruit cocktail ready for me to open and place in a bowl when the grandmother wakes up.* She's efficient, timid, and a little out of place in our boisterous home. Although Bubbe can't hear a word she says, it looks like Sandy can get the job done.

Marilyn is the primary caregiver, and you can hear what she is saying a block away, an ideal volume for Bubbe. Even when she is shouting, she manages to be kind, yet firm with Bubbe. I'm sure of this because wherever I am in the house, I hear every word she says, including her long, easy laugh.

When Bubbe doesn't want to get up, or walk to the bathroom, or get dressed, Marilyn says, "OF COURSE YOU WILL, HONEY, YOU HAVE TO. LET'S GO NOW. YOU DON'T WANT TO LIE IN BED ALL DAY, DO YOU, BUBBE?" Bubbe, who actually does want to lie in bed all day, since she's a hundred and three and a bit tired, feels the bulk of Marilyn's resolve, and usually goes along with the program. Last night I heard them cackling like a couple of old crones at midnight, so I went downstairs to see what was up. Marilyn pointed at Bubbe's bright red slippers while Bubbe squealed, "Da Bubbe in da red slippers!" as she shook her feet. This was followed by gales of laughter from both of them. When they caught their breath, Marilyn said, "NOW HONEY, YOU GO TO BED," and Bubbe did.

Karen, the weekend caregiver, looks Mediterranean with her olive skin and long dark hair. When she arrived to meet us a week before Bubbe's arrival, she stared past us at the Hebrew letters on the wall of David's office. Her hazel eyes grew huge as she announced, "I feel like I'm coming home." David and I smiled. We've heard this story before—she was raised in a Jewish home but had abandoned her Judaism years ago.

On her first shift she walked over to Bubbe, held her hand, gazed into her eyes, then basically stayed that way all weekend. She had to be reminded to shift Bubbe's position, clean her up, and change the wet sheets. "Love and contact are the main thing," I told her, "but we can't let her get bedsores."

With each new caregiver, I go over what Bubbe eats, which medications to give, how to move her, clean her, and how to fetch her apple juice when she asks for water. She calls for "vater" regularly, but spits and says, "Dis is terrible" when she tastes it. If you bring her juice instead, she's satisfied.

In the midst of the chaos, Bubbe remains at the center. When I come in, she grasps my fingers and rubs, as if pulling the warmth of my hands into hers, stirring the blood. Our foreheads tilt together until they meet, and my heart stretches. I'm reminded of the long nights with a cranky baby, when you're so sleep-deprived that you're beyond sanity, then just as you contemplate hurling the baby out the window, he looks up and gives you a gurgly smile. Your heart melts and you decide to keep him and nurse him for the eighteenth time on that sore, cracked nipple.

At the end of the week I force myself to go to a *Shabbat* potluck gathering at a friend's house. From sundown every Friday to sundown Saturday is a day of being, rather than doing. Unwind, rewind time. Tonight there is fresh challah bread, tabouli salad, vegetarian lasagna, and the hum of conversation.

People settle in around David as he offers an anecdote about Bubbe. "Bubbe has the power to demote me with one word," he says. "If I come in and sit down with her, she says, 'Here's da rebbi. Hello, Rebbi.' But if she sees me walking by without stopping in, she says, 'He's *supposed* to be da rebbi.'" David imitates Bubbe shaking her head and pointing disdainfully, as he repeats, "He's *supposed* to be da rebbi." Everyone chuckles. Except me.

I stare straight ahead, afraid that if I make eye contact, I'll start to cry. Someone says, "Debbie, could you tell us a story about your bubbe?" Everyone turns to hear something heartwarming from the storyteller.

"NO, I don't want to talk about my grandmother tonight." My voice is louder than I expected. "I can't talk about her. NO."

The next morning I ask David, "Was I rude?"

"Maybe," he says. "But people just don't get what you're going through."

My friend Judy, who directs an improv theatre troupe that I sometimes act in, calls on Sunday night. She's one of the few who know how much my life has changed in the last ten days. She listens to the recitation of my trials with Bubbe, then declares, "You need respite care. Come over."

"Tempting," I tell her, "but I can't. Rachel needs help with an art project, I promised Ari I'd drive him to his friend's house, and Marilyn wants to talk about Bubbe's medications."

"Rachel can get help from David, you can talk with Marilyn tomorrow, and drop Ari at his friend's on your way here. Jane and I are waiting for you in the hot tub. *Now.*"

Ten minutes later they greet me at the door with towels and a robe, then flank me on the couch; Judy rubs my neck, while Jane, another member of the improv troupe, massages my feet.

"I forgot to tell you, whenever anybody touches me I cry." I dissolve on the couch, weeping.

"Oh you can do better than that." Judy's a therapist when she's not directing theatre. "Nobody's stopping you. Let's hear it."

I feel my belly begin to tremble and the words slide up through an ache in my throat. I open my mouth and roar, "You betrayed me, you left me with all of this!"

I realize I've been keeping a lid on my anger at David, not wanting to risk an argument since he's my only support at home. Now I'm pulsing with rage.

"*Bringing Bubbe here was your big idea! You promised me you'd be there, you've abandoned me!*"

"That's more like it." Judy nods.

After a few minutes of bellowing, my body hums as if I've routed out a clogged drain. We soak in the hot tub. I let them rub my feet, fix me steaming soup, and serve it to me on china.

As I drive home the words echo in my mind, "You betrayed me! You abandoned me!" That feeling of abandonment is a familiar visitor, tucked just under my breastbone. Even though I've pointed the anger at David, I know it's not really all for him.

ten

Monday morning I hear Bubbe and Marilyn stirring, so I go downstairs to see what's cooking. It's oatmeal, and Bubbe is sitting up at the table mixing it around with her spoon.

"Eat your oatmeal. It's good for you!" Marilyn urges.

When Marilyn goes into the kitchen, Bubbe leans over and grasps my hand with her sticky fingers. She wrinkles her nose and says in a half-whisper, "It's good for me, but who vants it?"

Marilyn sweeps back in. "Don't you like oatmeal, Bubbe?"

"Honey, I don't know vat I like." She pushes the bowl towards me. "You hev it. It's good for you."

"I already had breakfast." I don't want to get into a food argument with Bubbe.

"You know, Marilyn, I think I remember she likes eggs or pancakes for breakfast."

"I thought the fiber would be good." Marilyn looks disappointed.

"Good idea, but we might as well give her what she likes."

What to feed Bubbe is a constant topic of debate. The other day Marilyn and the hospice nurse talked about giving her Ensure, a sort of milkshake-vitamin supplement, between meals. "What for?" I asked. I have to keep reminding everyone that she's one hundred and three and dying, so our goal is to make her a loving, cozy nest to leave this earth from, not boost her up with vitamins. It's hard for caregivers to think of "care" as anything other than extending life.

Bubbe pushes the oatmeal toward me. "You eat it. It dessn't go to vaste."

She has spit into the bowl a few times and stirred it with her finger. "I'll put it in the refrigerator and eat it later," I assure her. I slip into the kitchen and throw the food into the trash on the way out. When I was growing up, it wasn't so easy to avoid Grandma's food.

On a Sunday morning in 1959 my mother, father, JoAnn, Nancy and I walk through the door of my grandparents' house in North Hollywood past an alcove full of wool coats stuffed with mothballs and old photo albums where people live in black and white without smiling. The house is like my grandmother: worn threadbare, sturdy and staunch. The carpet is a flesh colored wool that was once soft and welcoming, but now it's tamped down, bare and clean as a dry bone.

We go and sit in the living room, where I try to get to the big, blue high-back chair first. It smells of dark velvet and my grandfather's whiskey. Grandpa is still in the garage, smoking cigars, so I can have the chair until Grandma yells at him to come in for lunch. She perches on the edge of the couch. "Youse kids look vonderful," she says. "So haw are you?" She doesn't wait for an answer. Her eyes dart toward the kitchen, where she's spent all morning gearing up. "Vell, how about some lunch?"

"We're not hungry yet, Grandma. It's only ten o'clock." I say this slowly, as if spelling it out to a young child.. My grandmother's eyebrows squeeze together as she lets loose a long-suffering sigh. She gets up and begins to set food on the dining room table. "I'll just put a few tings out," she says, "Maybe you'll get hungry."

We shuffle to the dining room table, where there is the same meal each time we come until she is a hundred years old. At the center is a large roast chicken, falling off the bone, greasy and plain. Grandma "dessn't eat salt," nor does she cook with it. The rice pudding is a clump of sticky white rice with raisins cooked into it. When I lift the raisins out with my spoon, they leave a deep amber stain.

I poke at the chicken, bring a morsel into my mouth, halt and return it to my plate. I pick the raisins out of the rice pudding, and suck them, one at a time, rolling them on my tongue to detect just a trace of dark sweetness.

My grandma taps her fingers on the table. "Hev some more chicken," she says. Tap Tap. "You're hardly eating anyting." Tap, tap. "Oy, it's not good, I overcooked it."

"No, it's fine, Grandma, but we just had breakfast."

"I made too much rice pudding. Nobody vants to eat it."

My mother's eyes are far off. Nancy and Jo Anne look bored and fidgety. I'm the only one who wants to please my grandma. I wish that just once my mother would look at her mother and say, "That tastes so good." The forks would stop scraping, the fingers stop tapping, and Grandma's face would soften.

"This is my second helping of rice pudding," I announce. "I want credit!" My sisters laugh, but Grandma frowns.

Dessert is date cake, dark and chewy, like old, dry bread sprinkled with powdered sugar. I play with it, pretending it's ancient mountains spattered with fresh snow. "Bring out more powdered sugar," I beg. I spoon heaps of it over my piece of cake, until I can't taste the brown crumbs.

When Grandma surveys the food left on the table, she shakes her head sadly, as if we have left her with a large, dead body. "Vat vill I do vit all dis food? It's a sin to vaste food."

My mother answers in a dull monotone. "You'll have it for lunch tomorrow."

"No." Grandma scowls. "My doctor says I dessn't eat too much. I made it for you. Vat am I gonna do?" When we're silent, she throws her arms up for a grand finale. "Children in Europe are starving," she announces, but no one answers.

After taking a week off from the middle school I've gone back, which gives me a glimmer of a normal routine. This morning, just as I'm about to leave for work, Sandy, who is scheduled to take care of Bubbe in a few hours, phones. Her voice sounds tinny and strained.

"Debbie. . ." she pauses, takes a breath. "Are *you* the one who is spreading rumors about me that I'm not worth ten dollars an hour?"

"What do you mean? I've never spoken to anyone about you, Sandy."

"You know exactly what I mean. . . You *know* what you have been doing to me." Her tone is so oddly sinister that I realize she's not herself.

"Sandy," I say, as coolly as I can, "calm down. Do you know who you are talking to?"

"Of course I do, and I know *you're* the one who was calling me all summer, harassing me, trying to get me to work for less money when your grandmother was here before."

"My grandmother was never here before," I speak softly, but I'm chilled by her strange accusations.

"I cannot work for you any longer." The phone clicks.

I hang up, shaking. This prim woman who came with impeccable recommendations and spotless white shoes is mentally ill. What would have happened if she'd had an episode like this while she was taking care of Bubbe?

After calling the school to say I won't be in today, I phone hospice to explain what happened. Even though I keep repeating that they must take her off their list of recommendations, they don't seem nearly as distressed by it as I am.

Bubbe is in my care today again while we try to find another new caregiver. I feel edgy, looking over my shoulder, imagining Sandy showing up to continue her rampage. If she could conjure up things in her mind and turn on us so quickly, what else is she capable of? I keep walking by the windows, like a dog pacing, trying to guard the house.

Rather than take another recommendation from the hospice agency for a caregiver, I call several friends for referrals, until I find Rene, a French-Canadian former nurse who has retired in Ashland. She has kind, blue eyes and keeps Bubbe's room sparkling clean. The books on Judaism that line the walls fascinate her, so she begins to read about Jewish holidays when Bubbe sleeps. She's boning up on Chanukah, which will be here in a few days. She tells us she's a devotee of a female guru in India. As long as she's nice to Bubbe, isn't schizophrenic, and can relieve Marilyn twice a week, that's fine with me.

Marilyn is here most of the week, Karen takes the weekends, and Rene relieves Marilyn now for Wednesday and Friday dayshifts. It seems like the right people have settled in to be with Bubbe, each with her own style, and everyone is adapting.

Marilyn takes no nonsense from Bubbe or anybody else. She's annoyed that Karen does things differently on weekends, feeds Bubbe different foods, and doesn't wipe the bed rails clean enough. When she comes back after her weekend off, she walks around clucking and shaking her head as she checks things, rants a little about this and that, then settles in to her post. Yesterday, when she walked in, Bubbe's eyes lit up. "I'm glad you came to see me," she said, as if Marilyn were a royal visitor. Marilyn leaned in close as Bubbe took her face in her hands, tracing it with her fingers. "I like your big face," Bubbe declared.

eleven

Baba Yaga the witch swooped down from the sky in her mortar and pestle. Thick black smoke swirled from her cape as she jumped into the clearing. My group of twelve sixth-grade storytellers are rapt as I tell the "Baba Yaga" story of "Vasilisa and her Magic doll." We're working on voices and gestures today. I scratch the air with imaginary talons and raise my voice to an ominous screech.

Bats and owls flew from her hair, and toads and beetles scurried from her feet. She clawed at the air with her long bony fingers and gnashed her iron teeth. Her nose, like a rainspout, quivered and sniffed at the air.

I used to picture a faceless crone when I told this story, but now I can't help but see Bubbe's sunken eyes and stiff, swollen fingers grasping at the air. Vasilisa, the brave heroine, has to face Baba Yaga and complete the impossible jobs set before her, with the help of her magic doll, a gift left to her by her mother.

I pull a little dark-haired doll from the pocket of my loose vest and tell my twelve students, "I've had this doll since I was little. She was getting dusty on a shelf until I found this story; then she jumped down and told me she wanted to help me tell it."

I remember my mother buying me this doll when I was seven. Unlike Grandma, who always wanted to get rid of things, my mom wanted to buy more than she needed and especially liked to indulge me because I was the youngest. That day she said if I helped with the shopping we could go the toy section and pick out a doll. I loved dolls. I loved to dress their smooth-jointed bodies in outfits and act out complicated scenarios in squeaky voices. It was a safe world of unbreakable faces, hinged knees, and eyes that blinked if you tipped them at just the right angle. I walked down an aisle of flaxen-haired dollars that day until I found one that looked like me, with dark, straight hair and soft brown eyes.

When Vasilisa faces her tasks in the story, I hold up the doll.

> Vasilisa fed the doll and she sang,
> "Here, Dolly, feed. Help me in my need
> Let me hear your voice so true. Tell me, Dolly, what am I to do?"
> The doll opened her eyes, and her eyes shone like candles. She sang back,
> "Do not worry, Vasilisa, Dear. Evening flies and morning will be near.
> Keep me with you and you'll know, I will show you where and how to go."

When I sing the words, my throat aches. I wish I could hear my own mother telling me where and how to go, but no matter how hard I listen, her voice is far away.

In 1980 my father and I sat, talking about my mother, sipping diet soda from bright colored cans, at the antique oak table that Bernice bought when they moved to the beach after my sisters and I were grown. Two years after the move, she died in her new bedroom, surrounded by the ocean view. My father lived twelve more years, often sitting at that table, staring into space. I could see his fuzzy reflection in the wood that he oiled and polished weekly, as if he could summon her forth with his slow, deliberate strokes.

That day, five years after her death, I asked him "Do you remember if mom breastfeed any of us?"

He held his face in his hands, elbows on the table, gazing straight ahead. "She tried to nurse JoAnn, but she didn't have enough milk. JoAnn cried all day and so did Bernice. It was terrible."

Even though it took five days for my breasts to fill after Rachel was born, I was told to be patient. But JoAnn was born in 1946, when nursing was an embarrassing bodily function being replaced by the clear, sterile bottle. I looked past my father's eyes to imagine them in those first days. I see JoAnn howling in frustration as she tries to grasp a nipple. My mother grits her teeth, then collapses in sobs. The relationship spiraled down from there. I never saw any affection between my mother and JoAnn. When my sister Nancy arrived less than two years later, Bernice had barely caught her breath. Her child-rearing books warned her not to slight JoAnn, who was a willful two-year-old with shiny ringlets, commanding all the attention in the room, so my mother hardly paid attention to Nancy.

"I just wasn't ready," she told me years later. "When Nancy was almost two I turned around and realized I had a little girl that I'd barely noticed." While my mother's head was turned, JoAnn gleefully terrorized her little sister. A photograph shows them in identical, puffy-sleeved dresses at five and three years old. JoAnn's hair bounces around her head in thick, corkscrew curls, but Nancy is virtually bald. A week before, JoAnn had played barbershop with her only customer, Nancy.

When Nancy was three and a half, I was born in the midst of two sisters at war, an angry mother who was starting to drink too much vodka on the rocks, and a quiet, sad father who buried himself in his work. In a photo at six months I stare at the camera, my mouth set in a determined line.

My mother told me, "You were such a good baby. You never cried. You talked in sentences at six months and you were toilet trained at a year. I didn't have to do anything!" It might be an exaggeration, but she got the basic idea right. While my mother and sisters raged at each other, I watched. I decided to be the good child.

When I was five my parents moved deeper into the suburbs and bought a tract house in the middle of the orange groves. Bernice fixed Caesar salads in her model kitchen while she read Haim Ginott on parenting. She stayed home until the day I went to first grade, then started a nursery school, where she became a self-styled guru on child development. Her secret dream was to have a college degree like her friend Ruth, who was a social worker. Once, when I was ten, rifling through her drawer, hoping for a glimpse of her birth-control diaphragm, I found a business card that read, *Bernice Gordon, MSW.*

When I walked home from elementary school each day, I looked for my mother as I rounded the corner onto Gledhill Street. I can see her now, standing in front of our tan stucco house, aiming the garden hose under the oleander bushes. She's as broad-shouldered and smooth-skinned as she was in her teens, but she's added sixty pounds. She carries it well, standing erect in a green shirtwaist dress and faux-pearl earrings. Her black hair is sprayed into a stiff hairdo that seems too tidy for her large, loose face. Her lips are lined with Avon Coral Frost. She turns to me, grins, and pretends to squirt me with the hose.

In those days I cringed because my mother was too large and too loud at PTA meetings, she refused to say "under God" in the pledge of allegiance, and talked to everybody in line at the supermarket. But if you had lined up all the mothers on Gledhill Street and asked me, "Which one looks the most alive?" I would have pointed to my mother.

⌒

When I come home from the middle school I hear David's voice downstairs. He's wrapped in his prayer shawl, sitting next to Bubbe, whose bed is cranked so high her face nearly touches his. It's hard to decipher what they're saying, since she sprinkles her conversation with Yiddish when she's with him, as if his beard and yarmulke trigger a switch into the old country.

They're discussing Hebrew names. When David says prayers for someone, he uses that person's Hebrew name. That officially includes their parents' names—so, in prayer I am *Devorah Bat Nachum V' Bracha*. Debra, daughter of Milton and Bernice. David is trying to get Bubbe's family names straight, so he can pray with her.

Bubbe closes her eyes and tips her head. "*Oivrum Yitzuk*," she says slowly. She bobs her head from side to side as if tapping into a hidden rhythm and repeats, "*Oivrum Yitzuk*."

When I look puzzled, David explains, "Her father's Hebrew name was *Avram Yitzhak*." He pronounces this carefully so I understand it's Hebrew for Abraham Isaac. I knew my great grandfather's name was Isaac. *Oivrum Yitsuk* is Bubbe's Yiddish version of his Hebrew name.

Bubbe's name is Lena, but if you ask what her Hebrew name is, she says, "*Soiralaya*," rolling the "R" with a soft, guttural sound like a mix of French and German. I thought *Soiralaya* was a one-word name, but David says that this is her version of "Sarah Leah."

"What was your mother's name?" David asks her.

Since her mother's name was Rose, I assume she'll say *"Shoshana,"* the Hebrew for Rose. But Bubbe says, *"Rukhel.* It vas *Rukhel."* This is the Yiddish version of Rachel.

Rachel. I never meant to name my daughter after Rose. We wanted to name her after my mother, who died six years before she was born, but we didn't want to give her the first name Bernice. When she arrived two and a half weeks before her due date, we'd been considering Rachel, but it wasn't final. She made faint "bleating" sounds through her first night, so we called her our little lamb. The next morning when David looked up the meaning of "Rachel," he found it was "Lamb of God." The choice was obvious. Rachel Bernice.

I would never have named my daughter after Rose, the cruel mother in my grandmother's stories, who beat her and made her take care of her siblings.

"Rukhel," Bubbe repeats, "my modder's name vas Rukhel."

"Bubbe," I tell her, gaping, "that's Rachel's name, my daughter, your great-granddaughter!" I shout so I'm sure she hears me, "RACHEL BERNICE! She has your mother's name *and* your daughter's name. I never knew that!"

Bubbe shrugs as if this is nothing new, and nods her head. *"Rukhel."*

twelve

Eight years ago, when Bubbe was ninety-five years old, we visited her at her house in North Hollywood. After dinner David pulled out our new camcorder. "Bubbe," I told her, "we want you to tell us about your life."

"My *life?*" She wrinkled her nose.

"That's right. Would you talk to me about it while David videotapes?" She shrugged. "Okay, but who'd vant to know?"

"We do." David aimed the camera and she began.

"Vell, I vas born in Russia a long time ago. I don't know, let's see, I'm vat? Ninety-five now, so it must have been . . . about eighteen-ninety-tree. It all seems like a dream. I don't exactly know ven vas my birtday, but it vas Rush Hashunna, de New Year, so later ven ve came to America, dey told us September 20, but who knows if dat vas da real date." Bubbe leans forward, elbows on the table, just warming up.

"Do you remember things that happened to when you were little?"

"Some tings you kent forget. Ve had to move a couple of times to get away from da Cossacks. Von day dey come into our house and tore it apart. Dey grabbed my aunt, my fadder's sister. I remember, I vas little so I vas hiding under the table. Dey pulled her and trew her down on the ground and dey broke her arm. She vas screaming, 'Yitsak, Yitsak!' to my fadder. But he vas on da ground, too. So dat vas the Cossacks, honey."

"Did you live in a Shtetl with other Jews?"

65

"No. Da village ve lived in vas called Grudna Gubernik. Dere vere hardly any odder Jews in de village. Dere vas von odder Yiddish lady dere, but my modder didn't get along vit her. My modder vas a tough voman, honey. She didn't like it if you said anyting or did anyting dat vasn't vat she vanted. If I did someting she didn't like, she didn't talk about it, she just hit. She beat, beat, beat."

I studied my grandma's face. When she talked about her mother, her jaw tightened as she looked away, avoiding my eyes. "Grandma, what do you think made your mother so mean?" I asked. "How'd she get that way?"

She drummed her fingers on the table, thinking for a minute. "Vell, she came from a rough femmily. My fadder's femmily, dey vas educated people, but my modder's femmily vas poor, dey didn't go to school and dey vas rough. My modder vas da only girl, so she hed to be tough like da boys."

"Did your father try to stop your mother when she hit you?"

Bubbe shook her head. "My fadder vas a good man, but he didn't dare say anyting to my modder. She vas alvays beating me, but he'd never say a vord. Vat could he do, honey? My modder ran da show. She vas smart. She heddn't gone to school and she couldn't write, but she vas a business voman. She signed her name vit an 'X,' but she did all da accounts by herself by adding tings up in her head. She ran a store, she bought a house, and she vas da boss of the femmily."

"And you took care of the other kids when you were little?" I'd heard these stories so many times, but I wanted to look again, to peer inside her words to see where she came from.

"My brodder Jack vas born ven I vas about six years old. Ven he vas just a few veeks old my modder hed to go avay for da whole day—some kind of business vit da court, like jury duty. Dey didn't hev bottles to feed da babies in dose days. She said to me, 'Take him to the lady who lives up da street, and she'll nurse him.'

"So after a vile he got hungry and he started to cry, so I took him to the lady, but she just slammed da door in my face and said, 'Go home. Tell your modder to take care of her own baby.' So, vat could I do? I hed to go home. He cried and he cried, my baby brodder Jack. Oy, he cried so loud I didn't know vat to do. So I took a little pumpernickel bread, and I mushed it into a little ball and I covered it vit a little demp cloth, and I let him suck on it till he fell asleep. Den ven he voke up, he screamed again because he vas so hungry, so I took some milk and I just dripped it into his mout vit a spoon. I vas only six years old myself."

As she spoke I watched Bubbe's thick fingers shape the mashed bread into a wad, curl the cloth around it, cradle the lump in her hand as if she felt her newborn brother sucking. I wanted to reach out and stroke her hands, make it okay, but the moment sat between us like a gaping sore.

The first week in December Ari's Language Arts teacher phones. "I'm a little worried about Ari," he says.

A knot forms in my stomach. "What's the problem?"

"All the girls cluster around him at every break."

"And?"

"Well, it's all the older girls. He's like their favorite toy. I don't really know if it's a problem, I've just never seen anything like it."

In the car on the way to school I tell Ari about it. He says, "So what?"

"So, I don't know. What would you say if the teacher called to tell you your twelve-year-old son was always surrounded by girls?"

"I'd say, 'That's my boy!'"

When I was pregnant with Ari I wondered if I'd have room in my heart for another child, but from the moment he was born I was crazy about him, much to Rachel's dismay. "I could be sick and vomiting on the floor," she says, "and you'd say, 'Oh, you'll be fine, get up and help me make dinner.' But if Ari so much as sneezes, it's, 'Darling, let me get you a Kleenex, may I wipe your nose for you? Let me fix you some soup. How about alphabet soup so we can play with the letters?'"

She's stretching it a little, but she has a point. Rachel, who has never been late to anything in her life, was born two weeks early, looking a bit worried, as if she'd landed in the wrong place. We fumbled with nursing for days, me not sure how to offer my rigid, swollen nipples, and she not able to get her tiny mouth around it all. Sometimes I think we're still trying to get that right. I see so much of myself in her; my mother, my sisters, the whole line of women who struggle to love each other.

The Language Arts teacher asks me to come help with the class play. Even though it takes hours everyday, it's a welcome relief from the dark, wood-paneled walls of Bubbe's room. They're putting on an adaptation of *The Giver*, a futuristic novel where everyone is controlled by the government. Ari plays Asher, the hero's friend. When he's given his "assignment" for his life's work, he finds out he's "Director of Recreation." Perfect type-casting. While Rachel will likely earn a Ph.D. in Ancient Literature or Anthropology, Ari will be happily skiing down a mountain slope somewhere.

"Soon you will have your first *strings*," declares the thirteen-year-old playing the mother as she gives advice to her son in the play. Her neon blue-streaked hair is stuffed into a kerchief for the role.

"Slow down," I direct her. "He's going to have '*stirr-ings*,' not '*strings*.'"

"What are *stir-rings*?" asks one of the sixth graders. The teacher smiles.

"It's when you start to like girls," says Ari.

On the night of the performance it all comes together: the scenery, the costumes, the lights—even the twelve-year-old pianist who's been in bed with the flu shows up at the last minute—and all the kids remember their lines, more or less. The parents are impressed and the teacher is grateful. If they only knew how simple this is compared to dealing with Bubbe.

Rachel, too, has landed a role in her school Shakespeare play, the *Comedy of Errors*. She plays Dromio, a manservant who wears an outlandish red wig and gallivants about the stage, ranting and raving. Rachel gets so exhausted from all the rehearsing that she comes down with strep throat halfway through the performances. She has to go on anyway, even with a fever and a throat like raw hamburger, so I bring her hot soup backstage, then sit in the audience exuding motherly empathy. When she slowly opens her mouth in mock-horror in one slapstick scene, I'm the only one who can see her swollen, red tonsils.

In the midst of all this, Chanukah arrives. This year it's December 6th, a little early for me. When it falls during Christmas break, there's more time to have friends over, play dreidle, and watch the candles burn slowly. This year we'll settle for lighting the menorah and singing a song or two.

When David and I began dating in 1978, neither of us had celebrated Chanukah in years. We were so estranged from our Jewish roots, that if you told me then that David would one day become a rabbi, I would have laughed my head off.

Three years after our first date, when Rachel was a week old, I opened the newspaper and read, "Chanukah Begins Tonight." Suddenly it mattered.

"Do we have a Menorah?" I asked David.

He crawled into our storage space and brought up a huge box.

"A Menorah that big?"

"It's just wrapped big." We peeled through layers of yellowed newspaper to uncover a hand-cast brass menorah from Jerusalem that had been handed down in his family for generations. We cleared a space on the hearth, set up the candles and sang the blessings slowly, holding our infant daughter close to the light.

We joined the little Jewish congregation in the Valley because we wanted connection to the community and our roots, but we had little connection to God. I went to High Holy Days services in the fall because the words of the prayers made me feel quiet inside. In those days David was too busy working to join me; he was teaching poetry, writing textbooks, and running his jazz club.

It wasn't until Rachel was seven and Ari almost five that David had a religious awakening. He'd spent two years on an album of children's poetry with music that ended up an award-winning product, but a financial disaster. After sinking our savings into it, we were broke and David was depressed. He began studying Torah with a local rabbi and going to services while he searched for something missing in his life.

When he dove into studying Judaism I was as bewildered as if he had a new woman in his life, and I felt my bias against religion rising. My father used to say, "All religious people are rigid, especially Orthodox Jews." He was probably talking about the stringent rabbis at the *cheder* he was forced to attend after school when he wanted to play football. Like so many Jews in the post-holocaust generation, my parents raised me to know my roots but not to be devout. Light candles at Chanukah, eat lox and bagels, but most of all, be American; blend in.

When David started wearing a yarmulke I was embarrassed. The handsome poet and businessman I'd married was morphing into a religious man with a scraggly beard. In those days, when I wasn't busy teaching, storytelling, and taking care of our kids, I was exploring my inner child with my women's group. For me, psychology was the route to personal growth, not religion.

I began to see changes in David, though. For the first time in years, his eyes filled with tears as he prayed and I sensed his softening when he sang Shabbat melodies, lit candles, and taught the children blessings.

On a chilly day in January, a year after he found Judaism, we sat on the couch. I said, "I was afraid we were growing apart, but I think it's okay now."

He nodded. "We've been on different paths."

"Yours is more spiritual, mine's more emotional, but I think we're headed in the same direction." I reached up and touched his face.

He covered my hand with his. "Are you through complaining about my beard?"

"Done."

Since he's become a Jewish Renewal rabbi, David's had room to create his own style, full of singing, poetry, and humor. He leads services with the same soft electricity as when he strummed the guitar in my second grade class. He's found his place.

I've slowly carved out a place at his side. When we went to Israel in 1990, I discovered Jewish stories called to me more deeply than the other folktales I'd been telling. These were my stories. Now I tell stories at services, create plays in our Sunday school, and lead women's rituals. On Friday nights when we light candles together and bless our children, I see the safety of the circle we stand in; Rachel and Ari know where they belong.

"If it weren't for you," I tell David, "I don't know if I would ever set foot in a synagogue."

He replies, "Then you're so lucky you married me."

The first night of Chanukah we carry our ancient brass menorah downstairs to light candles with Bubbe. Marilyn has gotten her dressed, fed, and up in the chair. She wears loose red sweat pants and a zip-up sweatshirt. Marilyn convinced me to buy her some clothes that are warm, comfortable, and above all, easy to get on and off. Last week I made a run to a local discount store and bought about ten jogging outfits. "Dis is nice," Bubbe says when Marilyn puts her in a new sweat suit. "But I don't tink it's mine."

She's pleased to see us coming in with candles and thinks it must be Shabbat. "No, Bubbe, tonight is the first night of *Chanukah*," Rachel tells her. She's anxious to go, has a six o'clock call for her play, but she leans down and gives Bubbe a big kiss.

"Chanukah! Ven did it get to be Chanukah?" Bubbe throws up her hands.

"It came early this year," David says.

We set the menorah in front of Bubbe, and I tell Ari to help her put the candles in it. When he has a specific job to do, he's more comfortable with her. He gently curls his hands around her fingers as they push in one candle for the first night of Chanukah, and the *shammos* candle to light the first one.

Ari lights the *shammos*, then hands it to Bubbe. Her hand shakes as she slowly finds the wick, and holds it until the flame flickers. We turn off the overhead light, so for a moment there is just that wavering, hopeful light as it joins the other, then grows stronger. When Bubbe says the Chanukah prayer in her thick Yiddish accent it sounds like a different prayer; *Broichatoi odonoi elehenu melechoilum*. The kids look quizzical, as if they've never heard it before.

David takes out his guitar and we sing "I Had a Little Dreidle." Bubbe croaks, "Dreidle, Dreidle, Dreidle," as she spins hers. When Ari points out the Hebrew letters on each side of the dreidle to Bubbe, he's surprised that she already knows what the letters mean: *Ness Gadol Haya Sham*, A Great Miracle Happened There.

Bubbe looks up at the dancing light, takes in the singing, and says, "I never vould hev believed I'd live long enough to see dis. To be here vit my grendchildren, and great-grendchildren, singing at Chanukah. Who vould believe dis? Ven I get home, I'm going to tell dem about all of you; dey're not going to believe dis."

thirteen

On the Wednesday evening before Winter break, Ari sidles up to me at the dining room table where I'm scratching out a chart of the caregiver's hours, and gives me a big hug.

I turn around and stare. "What's up?" Until this year we cuddled all the time, but now that he's twelve his body is a new zone. Hands off.

"I love you, Mom. Want to drive me over to Jenna's?"

"Actually, I do, if you go down and visit Bubbe first."

Rachel has become more relaxed with Bubbe. She pops in after school or on weekends, talking loudly, and giving lots of kisses. Ari, on the other hand, doesn't go unless forced.

"Do I *have* to?"

"No. Do I *have* to drive you to Jenna's?"

"I could walk, Mom!" It's about thirty-eight degrees outside and raining, hard.

"How about you just talk to Bubbe for a few minutes? She gets such a kick out of seeing you. Then I'll drive you."

He groans and shakes his head, then heads downstairs.

The door is open to Bubbe's room, so I watch from the top of the stairway as he sits down at her bedside, then positions his nose about even with the bedrail, and peers over the top.

Bubbe croaks, "Vell, hello."

"HI BUBBE, HOW ARE YOU?" I see Ari's eyes dart to the sliding glass door to the driveway, mapping his escape route, then back up to me. I smile encouragingly. Marilyn bustles in from the kitchenette, where she's been cooking macaroni and cheese.

"Look, Bubbe, you have a VISITOR, your great-grandson, ARI! Isn't that nice!" She squeezes Ari's arm. "How is middle school, Ari, are you making new friends?" I hiss at Marilyn from the stairs, gesturing her away with my hands. Ari looks back up at me nervously, like a trapped animal. He mumbles a few more words to Bubbe then scurries for the door.

After I drive Ari to his friend's, I come back downstairs where Marilyn sits in a chair reading while Bubbe naps. Her dog, Buddy, an aging brown lab-mix who she's started bringing with her, snoozes at her feet. Bubbe hums her faint groans, while Buddy wheezes in rhythm.

I sit down across from Marilyn and clear my throat. "I'm sorry I shooed you away when Ari was in here."

Marilyn glances up at me and looks down at her book again.

I pull my chair closer. " I just want Ari to be able to talk to Bubbe by himself so he can make his own relationship with her."

Marilyn nods. "I know. It's okay." But her eyes tell me I've hurt her feelings.

The same loud, motherly personality that makes Marilyn the ideal caregiver for Bubbe makes her a teenager's nightmare. When she leans into Bubbe and says, "DID YOU EAT ALL YOUR PANCAKES? IS IT TIME TO GO TO THE BATHROOM?" it works perfectly, but Rachel and Ari shy away from her "in your face" style.

When Rachel visits on weekends, Karen lets her have her own time with Bubbe. I have more free time on the weekend, too, so on Friday nights we all go down to light Shabbat candles with Bubbe and Karen. When Marilyn hears about this, she's jealous. She complains to me about how poorly Karen takes care of Bubbe, as if Karen were the preferred sister who gets more attention.

Marilyn looks up at me again. "Did you find somebody to cover for me this Sunday night?" When Karen takes the weekend shift, Marilyn returns on Sunday at five, but this week she wants more time off so she can go to the Rosh Hodesh gathering.

"I called Karen to see if she can stay late. She'll let us know."

"Couldn't you just fill in for a few hours if Karen can't?" Marilyn glares at me.

"I'm leading Rosh Hodesh. I have to go."

Marilyn sighs, long and slow. I know I can't make things perfect for her, anymore than I can for Bubbe, but her sigh makes me feel guilty. Buddy looks up from his post at her feet, yawns, and curls up a little tighter.

The next morning on the way downstairs I pause. The door is open so I can see Bubbe sitting quietly, her dark shape silhouetted against the window. Although her fingers are swollen stiff and her wrists spindly, she still grips the dreidle we gave her at Chanukah, spinning it on her table, again and again. When her hands are empty they shake, tap, and grab at the air. She rubs her fingers against each other, as if worrying a sore. When the dreidle is in her hand she grasps and spins, grasps and spins.

After she is up, dressed and has eaten, she sits in her chair, her hands fumbling around, reaching for something to connect to. When I was young, she was always cooking or sewing. In later years she would knit or crochet. As her eyesight dwindled and her fingers became stiff, the afghans she knitted were looser, more uneven, the colors louder. She kept on crocheting garish blankets, wooly berets, and mismatched slippers that seemed made for alien creatures until she couldn't see the stitches and her fingers were too numb to make the crochet hook fly.

When I would visit her house, she would whisper, "Come to the beck bedrum," as she led me down the hallway. The back bedroom knew no era. My cousin Marcie's princess furniture from the '60s, a pink and white glossy painted dressing table and chair, was crammed in with a dark, heavy sleigh bed from the '30s.

Grandma was always prepared for visitors, her offerings spread over the bed. Dishtowels with gaudy crocheted handles, odd-shaped hats, loopy scarves, and purple slippers. Next to those were are the old things—my mother's outsized 1950's handbag, Aunt Minnie's wool coat with a fake fur collar, and giant clip-on rhinestone earrings.

"Here," she murmured, as she pressed dishtowels into my hand, yellow with bright red acrylic trim. "Kent you use dese?"

As a teenager, I'd refuse it all. The stuff in the back bedroom was sticky with whispers, unfulfilled longing. Later, in my twenties, I began to take bags of it. Why not, if it made her happy? I'd stuff it into my Volkswagen and drive it back to Oregon, where I'd unload some of it at the Goodwill, then stash the rest in my closets. Strange, musty crocheted things and crumpled purses would tumble off the shelves when I opened the doors. Sometimes I'd finger them, like an old letter from home, then cram them back in.

No matter how much I took it never pleased Bubbe any more than pointing out how much rice pudding I'd eaten. "Oy, honey," she'd plead, "Couldn't you take some more?"

Now, when I sit with her she tips her head into mine, takes my hands, and rubs and strokes, rubs and stokes. When she's alone, she grabs and spins the dreidel, lets it wobble and drop, then spins it again.

Diane, the hospice nurse, who visits every Tuesday afternoon, finally brings the morphine cream that Dr. Rose ordered for Bubbe. To get a medication that isn't on the approved list took four weeks and about twenty phone calls. She hands me the tube with a bill for $96.00.

I look at her blankly. "I thought hospice covers all of the medications."

"Oh no," Diane says crisply. Her blond hair is coifed just so, and her nylon stockings are smooth above red pumps. No scuffs. She looks out of place in Bubbe's room, where we scurry around in sweatpants scrubbing away the tinge of death. "We don't ever cover medications that aren't on our list."

It's been a constant scramble to find the right combination of drugs to ease Bubbe's back pain, control her hacking cough, and at the same time keep her bowels going. Last week we tried codeine tablets only when she complained of pain, and one laxative a day. She ended up constipated and groaning. This week we put her on codeine every four hours, complaining or not, plus two laxative pills, prune juice, and an antacid. Less pain, but diarrhea.

The biggest problem is getting Bubbe to swallow anything. She glowers at medicine and declares, "Dat don't do nuttin'." We've learned not to hold any bottle too close, since she can swipe at it so fast that we've all been drenched in sticky cough syrup. Sometimes she takes a pill, pretends to swallow and then spits it out later into her Kleenex. If she were a better shot, we'd never know. We find half-dissolved pills floating in gobs of saliva wedged between her pillows, or crystallized on the back bedrails. We've been hopeful that rubbing the cream in regularly will be a simple way to quell Bubbe's constant squirming from pain.

"But Diane, you didn't tell me about the charge," I protest. I like Diane. She offers a kind, listening ear and a cool organization to this crazy, multi-layered project. But I don't remember her saying anything about an extra charge.

"I thought you knew." Diane shakes her head. She might have told me, and I missed it, but it's too late now that the bill has arrived with the cream.

Fifteen minutes after Marilyn gently rubs the white goo into Bubbe's chest, she becomes agitated. She waves her hands and shakes her head, twists her fingers, wants to be up, then down, and seems to constantly itch at nothing.

We give the cream a try for a couple of days, to allow time for side effects to diminish, but they don't. Two days later Bubbe twitches like a mechanical doll. Her hands spin her dreidle, then claw at the air as she rattles out a stream of words, then jerks around to see who is there. Her half sentences hang in the air and she looks startled, searching for their source. She doesn't recognize anybody and hollers at everyone.

"This is not working," Marilyn announces, holding out the tube of cream. She's right, of course. I write a check for $96.00 to hospice, and throw the tube into the trash.

After a few days off the cream, Bubbe is calming down. When I come downstairs I see she's still twitching and shifting around in her bed, but her eyes focus on something that she holds in her arms. As I get closer I see it's a yellow, stuffed lion.

"Where did that come from?" I ask.

"Sarah brought it for Bubbe when she visited today. Isn't it CUTE? BUBBE LOVES IT. DON'T YOU?" Marilyn makes the lion hop up and down on Bubbe's chest. Bubbe's head sways as she follows the dance.

Sarah is an elderly woman from our congregation. When Bubbe arrived we suggested people visit to give her company, relieve the caregivers, and offer community members a chance to do a mitzvah. Who could refuse?

Nearly everybody. Bubbe's like an alien creature, hovering between two worlds. Pulled toward death, her skin sags, her body reaches heavily to the grave, but her eyes are sharp and darkly alive. I'm getting used to those deep eyes, but others shy away. Good friends that I thought would have visited by now haven't shown up. It's as if we have something secret and contagious hidden in our basement. This is one of the biggest differences between a new baby and a new Bubbe. Everyone is eager to marvel at a sweet, moist, new baby; we love to touch the soft, fresh skin and smell the innocence. On the other side is wizened flesh and gnarled, gangly bones that remind us too sharply of where we're headed.

The first few weeks there were a dozen people who dropped in from the congregation, but now just a few regulars come a couple times a month: Charu, an eighty-year-old artist who draws pictures with Bubbe; Steve, a sweet middle-aged man whom Bubbe adores because she thinks he's her grandson Tommy; Jackie, a student Rabbi; and Sarah, who brought the stuffed animal today.

Marilyn tucks the lion back into bed, where it looks absurd, furry and grinning, next to Bubbe's droopy face. Bubbe gazes at it and mumbles.

Marilyn says. "She thinks it's her baby." Then she motions for me to sit down, and whispers, "Sarah thinks Bubbe needs more stimulation."

"Meaning?"

"She says Bubbe's bored, so we should give her tasks, like folding towels or something."

I stare at Marilyn. In my mind I see Bubbe flinging towels around, while Marilyn and I scurry around the room to fetch them. I swallow the urge to snap back, *Tell her to mind her own business!*

I take a deep breath, and as the flash of anger fades, I feel tears choking my throat. I speak slowly. "I think we're doing all we can for Bubbe. The morphine cream made her agitated, but she's coming out of it now."

Marilyn shrugs. "Sarah thinks we should read her books and play music and make more things for her to do."

My shoulders slump, as if I've been given a lousy progress report. *The nursing home director has neglected to provide adequate recreation for her patient.* I straighten up and squeeze my hands tight in my lap. "Well, Sarah isn't here every day. Bubbe gets a lot more love and stimulation here than she ever did alone in her house, or in that awful nursing home."

Marilyn nods. We both know this is true. I get up from the table, but my legs are quivery, and I realize I've been digging my fingernails into my palm to keep from crying. *Why can't I ever do it right?* A numbness, a sense of failure, sits just under my skin. It's like the dark futility behind Bubbe's eyes, or the deadness I heard under my mother's sigh before she sipped a martini.

⌒∽

It's 1963. I'm twelve years old and it's four o'clock, any day of the week. My mother and her friend Ruth are about to arm themselves with a pitcher of vodka martinis and settle into the living room to take the edge off their suburban afternoon. My mother stands in the kitchen gathering supplies: a giant economy-sized bottle of Smirnoff's, olives for Ruth, cocktail onions for herself, and a dash of vermouth. She wears a pair of Bermuda shorts and sandals, and her make-up is smudged from a day at the playground where she teaches preschool. When the phone rings I grab it. "Hi, Ruth," I say as I hand it to my mom who is gesturing impatiently. "My house today," she says.

Ruth is at the door in three minutes flat. The Brudneys are our best friends, and they live right across the street in the Storybook Lane subdivision. We live in the Cinderella model with the kitchen in front and four bedrooms. The Brudneys have the Peter Pan, with only three bedrooms, but a real family room where Bonnie and I watch cartoons on Saturday mornings and *The Twilight Zone* on Thursday evenings.

"Hi, Bea," Ruth calls as she sails into the house without knocking, crackers and cheese tucked under her arm. She is much smaller than my mom and about ten years older. Her thick, prematurely white hair is sprayed into a stiff coif just above her ears. She had her children in her thirties, because she waited until she had a career. She's a social worker with a master's degree, which means that my mother looks up to her and hangs on every word she says.

They're about to say a lot of words in the living room, more and more as the vodka flows. They won't chat about events of the day, or titter over personal tidbits. As they sip, Ruth and Bea will psychoanalyze everyone they know, spare none.

Bonnie and I have a choice to make at Cocktail Hour. We can either hang out in the house where our mothers are drinking and eavesdrop, or we can escape to the empty house across the street and be blissfully unsupervised for over an hour. If we go, we're free to experiment with eye shadow, eat Hostess Twinkies, call boys on the phone, or read sex manuals, knowing that nothing will keep our mothers away from their martinis.

If we stay, we can monitor the collective unconscious of our mothers' friends, and since we know most of them, it can get interesting. Last week we learned that Nora, the cleaning lady's daughter, has difficulty relating to her peer group due to being the only child of a mother who is prone to hysteria and a father who lacks personal force. This was followed by an explanation of how Sandra, my friend Laurie's mother, is a compulsive eater because her husband is in love with her daughter—a clear-cut case of emotional incest. I'm a little bit embarrassed when I see Laurie now, knowing this inside secret, but it makes her seem exotic to have a fancy label attached to her family disorder.

I have no idea that there is a name for my family disorder. If you had told me then that my mother was an alcoholic, I wouldn't have believed it. Alcoholic is a word used for people who scream at their children, and drink all day. People who have no education, who vomit in gutters, and don't have jobs or nice houses, or sit in living rooms and use long, complicated words. Cocktail Hour is just a ritual that gets our moms over the slump and on with the day. Every day.

Today Bonnie has baseball practice, so I place myself in the kitchen and pretend to be doing my homework. My mother is talking about the man who supervises the playground where she runs her preschool. "I can't do a thing without him strutting around and giving an opinion! I try to soothe his little ego, but I just don't have the time for this," she says.

"It sounds like a Napoleon Complex," Ruth offers.

"Hmm, exactly." I can't see my mother's face, but I know she's nodding, agreeing, as she always does, with Ruth's diagnoses. I hear them pour refills from the pitcher, so I know they're on their second drink, and the words will slide faster, the laughter easier.

"How is the happy couple?" Ruth is referring to my sister JoAnn, a senior in high school, and her boyfriend, Greg, who's been home from college for spring break.

"They can't keep their hands off each other. The repressed hormones are flying around the room." They both laugh at this as if it were the punch line of a hilarious joke. My mother goes on, "I think they've come to a point in the relationship where they'll either have to break up or get married."

She means that they'll either break up to avoid having sex or get married to make it legal. What she doesn't know is that they already do have sex on the couch that Ruth and Bea are lounging on now. Last week I woke in the middle of the night to sounds of grunting and moaning. Confused, I walked down the hallway and saw JoAnn and Greg gyrating on the couch in front of the fireplace. Maybe my mother does know, but she'd never tell Ruth. Ruth doesn't approve of premarital sex; in fact she doesn't approve of sex at all. She and her husband, George, sleep in twin beds. I know my mother likes sex, because when my father comes home from work and kisses her, she presses her body into his and sighs. But she pretends not to approve for Ruth's sake. We have a whole set of rules that my mother has borrowed from Ruth. *No calling boys on the phone. No dating until sixteen. No closing the door if a boy is in your bedroom.*

They go on to talk about sublimating urges, and repressed grief. Greg's father died a year ago, and they're sure that his affection for JoAnn arises from this tragedy, combined with her need to mother and control, as the oldest child. I've heard this one before. At this stage they will recycle old conversations, throwing out snippets of used sentences as they delve into the third drink. I hear them sloshing their fingers into their glasses to fish out the ice. My mother cracks it loudly with her teeth. By the end of the third drink, they've dispensed with most of the verbs and conjunctions in their normal speech. Just the core words remain, but they understand each other perfectly. They're talking about Greg's mother, who may become an in-law. "Lovely she is," my mother says.

"Warm and relating," adds Ruth.

"Warm and relating," my mother echoes. The liquor sloshes, spills, the ice cracks. They are trying to tidy up, regroup, but they can hardly stand. My mother calls out to me, "Deb, did you make the salad?" Every night we eat steak or lamb chops or something that can be broiled quickly without any fuss. My sisters and I take turns making the salad.

"I'm going to do it now." I scramble off my seat as my mother lists into the kitchen. She leans on the counter for a moment to get her balance, then pulls the steaks out of the fridge, dousing them with a splash each of red wine and Wishbone dressing. Her wrists are limp, and she slops some of it onto the counter. As I wash the lettuce, I stare into the sink, then reach over and slowly wipe up her mess.

She will recover her speech sufficiently to get through dinner, then go to bed early with a book that will soon drop onto her chest as she dozes. Tomorrow morning she'll get up and light her first Lucky Strike at six forty-five A.M. with a cup of strong coffee and get to the playground before I go to school. At four o'clock she will go across the street to Ruth's house.

Ruth will die of cancer in four years and my mother will be dead in ten. A year after her death, for a writing assignment in college, I will write a funny story called "Cocktail Hour," and when I'm finished I'll put down my pen and begin to sob. "I watched you drink your life away," I'll say, as if I could see the vodka pouring into her and washing out her days.

fourteen

For New Year's Eve we're going out for a dinner with friends, like normal people without Bubbes in their basements do. Before we leave, I order a Thai dinner for Marilyn and bring it downstairs. I want her to feel appreciated since she's shut in with Bubbe so much. Since last week when I told her I couldn't find anyone to fill in on Sunday night, she looks away when I come in the room, as if she's hiding her anger. She smiles when I bring in the take-out dinner, though, and settles in to watch her favorite show, "Doctor Quinn, Medicine Woman," while Bubbe dozes.

Downtown, we gather round a large table, five couples all dressed up, eating gourmet food. This is the kind of restaurant where each plate is a work of art: lamb ribs propped to look like exotic flowers; sauces swirled into abstract patterns. I drink champagne until I'm lightheaded and laugh at jokes that aren't funny.

An old friend, a poet, leans close to me. "I wish I could make more time to write," he confides.

"You will," I announce, peering into his champagne glass. "I can see it clearly in the bubbles. This is the year for you because you truly want it. You'll see."

We laugh about me not being able to accomplish anything this year with Bubbe running me ragged. Suddenly he locks eyes with me, takes my hand and says, "Bubbe has something to give you."

I stare back, slightly sobered. "What do you mean?"

"I'm not sure, but it's something important. It's not just her soul that needs you. You need her healing, too. She's going to give you something."

My stomach suddenly feels queasy. Too much champagne on top of rich food. "I hope so," I tell him.

When we finally stroll out of the restaurant, the water on the sidewalks is swirling up to our ankles. It's been pouring for a week and now it's obvious that a flood is imminent. This happens in Southern Oregon every twenty years or so, but we're never prepared for it.

The next morning, New Years Day, downtown Ashland is mostly under water. The creek that runs through Lithia Park has swollen into a river that courses through the streets, knocking down pine trees and park benches, and drenching businesses. The increase in water pressure has broken the city pipes, so we don't have running water and can't flush toilets. Last night Karen accidentally gave Bubbe two laxatives instead of one. Bubbe then provided her own flood of diarrhea, which we flushed down the toilet by pouring in pails of water siphoned from our neighbor's overflowing backyard pool. David ran back and forth with buckets half the night.

This morning we hauled everything out of my office since the floor is covered with two inches of water and lugged the furniture up to the only place it would fit—our living room. I've been saying that I have no room to move, but now the living room is jammed, my story files are buried, and there's no tap water. My Grandpa Morris used to smirk if one of us kids would cry. "You want to cry?" he'd say, "I'll give you something to cry about." *You thought you were crowded with Bubbe? I'll show you crowded.*

Karen was puzzled because Bubbe was up most of the night repeating, "Jeck and Jill vent up da hill to fetch a pail of vater." Marilyn says, "Oh, it's simple. That's because we always recite nursery rhymes before we go to bed. She just misses me and our bedtime rhymes." Actually, it's even simpler. Bubbe was just reporting what she sees: A parade of people carting pails of water in and out all day to flush the toilet.

The headline this afternoon in *The Ashland Daily Tidings* reads: "Flood Causes Schools to Remain Closed an Extra Week." I squint, turn it sideways, close my eyes, then open them. "Oh God, this can't be true."

Ari races into the kitchen. "Who are you talking to, Mom?"

"The newspaper." I point to the headline.

"Yes! I love this flood!" He grabs the phone and runs upstairs.

I don't love this flood; I'm drowning. There's no place to sit down in my living room. With school canceled I can't go back to work and the kids will be home in the cramped house for another week. I feel like a displaced refugee wandering through mazes in a house that no longer fits. I bump into the walls, bump into Bubbe, turn and bump into myself.

It seems futile to try to get my family to visit Bubbe more often. When I asked David this morning if he'd stop in to see her between meetings, he said, "I can't. I'm just too busy." I wanted to say, *You can't, you're just too selfish,* but I kept my mouth shut.

Ari hollers down the stairs, "Hey, Mom, where are my ski poles? I can't find them anywhere!"

"Good luck!" I snap back. "I can't find *anything* anywhere!" I don't bother asking him to visit Bubbe. He always refuses, saying, "I didn't want Bubbe to come here. Why do I have to visit her? It's boring." Probably what he means to say is, *She scares me and I don't know how to handle that.*

Usually I tell him, "It's a *mitzvah*. She loves to see you and we need you to help, to be part of the family." What I want to say is, *Goddamnit, you selfish little brat! All you ever think about is yourself.*

I don't know what to do with myself. Can't go to work, can't find a place to be. Even when I'm upstairs I sense Bubbe sitting in her room, fiddling with her dreidle, staring into space. Before she came I worried her visit would stir up the ugly feelings that simmer under the family skin. Now as she spins her dreidle, I feel as useless and bitter as she is. It's the same kind of bitterness I heard in my mother's voice when she spoke to her mother. Maybe this is what I was afraid to feel.

꧁

We're gathered around the white Formica dinner table in 1963, eating steak and salad in our orange flowered chairs. I'm eleven, Nancy is fifteen, and JoAnn almost seventeen. My mother, as usual, has had too many martinis with Ruth and is concentrating on sitting up in her chair and cutting her meat, which seems to slide around on her plate, out of control. JoAnn glares at my mother, who doesn't seem to be listening as she explains that her prom shoes don't match her prom dress so they'll have to be re-dyed till they're magenta, not fuchsia. Nancy, who isn't going to the prom, scoots her chair close to my father, who looks up from his food and smiles at her.

When the phone rings my mother nearly slips off her chair as she swivels round to answer it. "Hello." The word slides around her mouthful of steak. She leans hard into the counter as her voice flattens to a tense staccato. "Oh . . . Hello." We can tell from her voice who's on the phone, and there's a collective grimace, as if everyone has bitten into something rancid that we have to chew silently.

"We're having dinner now, Moth-er," she says, but she sounds like she's holding her breath to keep from inhaling a foul odor.

"No . . . No . . . You do NOT have to call back." She controls each syllable, coating it in ice. "It's O-kay, Mo-ther."

I look at the taut corners of my mother's jaw and remember the sound of the ice cracking after she drank her vodka. *Smash. Crunch.*

"Of course, Milt is home. It's sev-en o-clock, Mo-ther. The girls are all here. Why WOULDN'T they be?" Her voice is tight, like a rope stretching.

I look back and want to put the scene on pause. I'd like to reach in and touch my mother's throat until her voice softens. I scan to my sisters. JoAnn the narcissistic queen and Nancy, with her wounds just under the surface. I don't want any of them. I don't want Rose's rage, or Lena's fear, or my mother's tight jaw. I want to loosen the knots so when my daughter is grown she doesn't hold her breath when she speaks to me.

"No, I DON'T have a headache." My mother pronounces each word carefully, with exaggerated patience, as she sneers into the phone. "I . . . DON'T . . . get . . . headaches . . . anymore . . . Mo-ther."

Oh, yes she does. She's lying.

⌒

Aunt Derril calls in the middle of the week. "I heard there was a flood," she says. "Is everybody okay?"

"We're surviving."

"Can I tell Bubbe Happy New Year?"

I explain that we've given up putting Bubbe on the phone since she gets confused when she can't hear, so Derril asks me to send her love.

"That was Derril on the phone," I tell Bubbe.

She's sitting at the table eating pancakes drenched in syrup. She stares at each piece, toys at it with her fork, then stabs it before bringing it to her mouth. She glances up at me and stabs another bite.

I sit down so I'm in earshot. "DERRIL SENDS HER LOVE."

"Det's nice."

Marilyn moves in to wipe the syrup off Bubbe's face and fingers. She scowls like a child in a high chair putting up with Mom. "THAT'S NICE THAT YOUR DAUGHTER CALLED," Marilyn says.

"My dodder called?" Bubbe licks her lip to get the last of the syrup, then pushes back from the table and stares at me. "My dodder?"

"Yes, DERRIL." Bubbe's face is blank, so I get out some photos, turn her chair away from the table and point to a picture. We go over who her children are, who is gone, Sol, Merwin and Bernice, and who is left. Minnie and Derril.

"Derril and Norm, dey vent to live in Colorado." Bubbe shakes her head sadly as if this were the far corner of the earth. I remind her that they moved to San Diego last year, but she shakes her head again and corrects me, as if *I* am deaf. "COLORADO."

I nod. At least she's remembering that she has a daughter. Then she looks at me quizzically. "Vere are your sons?"

"I have a son and a daughter, Bubbe. Ari's out skiing and Rachel's upstairs."

"Oh, det's right. A dodder, too. Is she big enough to go to school?"

"She's big enough. She's FIFTEEN."

Bubbe drops her jaw and stares at me. "Ven did she get to be fifteen?"

This is a question I ask myself a lot these days. Being fifteen means that she finds one reason after another to argue with me. Last night at eleven she announced that she had to go to the bathroom. Since we have no running water that means going outside in the bushes if you have to pee, or going to one of the temporary porta-potties set up around town if you really need a toilet. She needed a toilet.

"It's too late to go out," I told her. You can use our toilet and we'll flush it with a bucket of water, like we do for Bubbe." We have special permission from the city since Bubbe is bedridden.

"I can't do that! It's bad for the sewage system."

"It's eleven o'clock. One time won't matter."

It's no use arguing with Rachel when her mind is made up. She dug in her heels and ten minutes later I sat in the car in the dark university parking lot, waiting for her to use the outhouse. I was pretty sure she no longer had to go. When she emerged, I silently drove her home, where she stomped up to her room.

"Did she do her thing?" David asked.

"I don't know," I told him, "but she made her point."

Today she's upset because we won't let her go to India to work in an orphanage for the summer. We tell her she can go after her senior year, but she's devastated.

"I'm old enough now! You don't trust me at all!" She was sobbing when I went down to see Bubbe.

Bubbe stares at me. "Naw, Rachel kent be fifteen. She's little." I go over to the stairs and call Rachel to come down.

Her eyes still red and swollen, Rachel walks down reluctantly. She ignores me pointedly, kneeling down to Bubbe's eye level. "*Hi, Bubbe,*" she says.

"This is Rachel, my daughter, your great-granddaughter," I announce.

Bubbe strokes Rachel's hair. "Look haw beautiful you are."

Rachel kisses Bubbe and declares, "I LOVE YOU."

Bubbe stares, like she's seeing a vision. "Look haw beautiful she is, da long dark hair, dese beautiful dark eyes."

"YOU'RE BEAUTIFUL, TOO." Rachel gently traces a line on Bubbe's cheek and beams at her.

When Rachel goes back upstairs Bubbe stares at the ceiling, her hands jerking as though she's adding up a list in her head, calculating with her fingers. Finally she balls up one fist and lets it settle into the other hand. "Naw I see it," she says.

"See what?"

"She's your dodder. I'm your grandmodder . . . she's your dodder." Her eyebrows have moved up almost to her hairline, and her eyes are huge, rising from their sunken state for this revelation. "Naw I see it. I see da connection."

I blink back at her. I hear Rachel clomping up the stairs, each step thudding, as if in slow motion. My mother gazes up at me from the photo in Bubbe's lap. I nod. "I see it, too."

fifteen

November, 1988

We've been sitting at Grandma's kitchen table in North Hollywood with the camcorder for over an hour. Bubbe's on a roll.

"When did you come to America?" I ask.

"I vas tvelve years old, I tink it vas in 1905. My fadder vent over first to live vit a cousin in Minnesota. Den he sent for us, so my modder and me and my brodders—Al, Jack and Joe—vent over."

"Didn't you tell me once that your brothers were sick on the trip?"

"My brodders came down vit de measles and my modder knew dey vouldn't let us on da boat. So she covered dem up vit coats so you couldn't see de red spots on dere faces and ve carried dem onto da boat." Grandma imitates her mother, pulling her hands over her face. Her eyes peer out and I see her brother's eyes, red-rimmed and frightened.

"Do you remember the boat?"

She nods slowly, as if she watches a faint movie in her head. "Oy, it vas crowded and it smelled. You don't vanna know how it smelled, honey, and lots of people vere sick, and dere vas hardly anyting to eat. I never vanted to go on a boat after dat."

"What happened when you got off?"

"Ve vent to a man at a vindow and he put a chalk mark on my brodder's jeckets. Dat meant dey vere sick. But my modder viped off de mark and

88

vent to da next vindow. Ven de man at de next vindow marked dem, my modder viped it off again. Ven ve came to de last vindow, dat man said. 'De children kent go vit you, de hev to go to a huspitel, so de von't infect da whole city.'

"Vell my modder started in. You shoulda herd my modder." Grandma wags her head and pounds her fist on the table as she launches into an imitation.

'HAW CAN DE INFECT DA WHOLE CITY? Ve're not going into da city! Ve're going to an apartment, and ve're gonna call a doctor! You can't take my kids. If dey stay here, den I stay too!' My modder kept yelling until dey finally just let us go."

I can see my great-grandmother with her broad face and massive chest, planting herself in front of the official and hollering to protect her children, to stay with them. I want to ask my grandma if she thinks her mother would have fought as fiercely to stay with her, her only daughter, but I'm afraid of the answer. We shake our heads silently as the question floats, unspoken.

"Where did you end up?" I ask.

"Ve vent to live vit my fadder's cousin in Minnesota. Ve hed to sleep in da kitchen—all six of us on da floor. Vun day I come home to da house ve vere staying in, but my modder vasn't dere. My cousin said, 'Mamma moved to anodder house.' She heddn't even told my fadder. So ve hed to go find da new house, and she vas all moved in."

"How did she do that, without any money?"

Grandma rolls her eyes. "My modder vas smart, and if she made up her mind, dere vas no stopping her, honey. She met a man and she made a deal. He'd loan her a hundred dollars if she'd pay him back tree dollars a mont for tree years. Det vas my modder. She borrowed furniture so it vas all fixed up ven ve got dere, like ve'd alvays been dere."

We both laugh as Bubbe closes her eyes and repeats. "Modder moved to anodder house!" I smile, thinking of my great-grandma's determination, her independence. I see that same solid stubbornness in my grandma, but I know the story is about to turn ugly, the laughter sour.

"You went to work at a factory, right?"

"I verked at 'Kepital Suspenders.' I set at a sewing machine sewing elestic for twenty-five cents a day. Den I'd come home and do all da housevork.

My chums at vork, dey esked me to go out vit them but I said, 'I hev to go home and clean da house.' Von day von of dem said, 'Tell your modder you'll clean up ven you get home. Vat can she do to you?' Oy honey, vat she could do, dey didn't know. But I vas tired of never going out like da odder girls; I vas about sixteen years old. So I told my modder, 'I'll clean up everyting ven I get home.' Of course she knew I vould because I alvays cleaned everyting. She said, 'No, you kent go.' But I vent anyvay.

"Ven I got home she took a lead pipe off of da heater register, she pulled it off and she beat me vit dat pipe till I tought I vas dead. I couldn't sit down for a veek. I never forgave her for dat. You know, I said to myself I vould never hit any of my children."

I gaze at my grandma. She didn't hit her children, but she bore her mother's rage like a heavy body part, that stooped her before she was old. She couldn't erase the sting of her mother's blows. The anger festered, shapeshifted, slid along, burst forth, and found new carriers who breathed it in, exhaled it, swallowed it cold, or drank it to death.

Dr. Rose calls to check on Bubbe's medications. When Marilyn tells her it was the doctor on the phone, Bubbe scowls and declares, "Too many doctors." She stretches her puffy fingers, then begins counting out. "A doctor for dis, a doctor for dat, anodder doctor for dis, and dey can't do nuttin'." She taps her fingers for each one and then repeats it from the top. "Too many doctors. A doctor for dis, a doctor for dat." Sometimes she gets into a rhythm with a phrase, like a needle stuck in a groove. She keeps this up for an hour or so, bobbing her head in time with the chant.

Marilyn pulls me aside and says, "I think Bubbe is psychic." I raise my eyebrows. In Ashland everybody believes in new-age healing, and good vibrations.

"Marilyn waves a magazine in front of my face. The article she's been reading is titled "Too Many Doctors."

I laugh. "You must have read the title so she overheard." Marilyn swears she never said it out loud. Besides, Bubbe's so deaf she can't hear unless you're a few inches away and hollering.

Bubbe's radar is definitely tuned to a wavelength below the surface. Whether she intuited anything from the article or not, she is saying something in her own way. Earlier today, when offered a pill, she announced, "No medicine. It don't do nuttin." We rush to try remedies when she winces and groans, but she knows most medicines don't help her. They make things worse, like the morphine cream that made her batty. Nothing, not drugs or "Too Many Doctors" who can't do "nuttin" can stop the progress of her tumor, blot out her pain, or cancel her death.

A week after the flood we still don't have running water. I've cleared a pathway through the maze of our crowded living room so I can I push past my printer, perched on top of my file cabinet, between two stacked office chairs, to get to the top of the stairway. I drag myself downstairs to check on Bubbe this morning, who stares at me, feels my fingers, and pronounces, "You're tired, honey."

It's as if she sneaked up and punched me in the stomach. Growing up, if I had the sniffles, she'd say, "Oy, I hope you get better," with a deep sigh as if I had leukemia.

I take a slow breath. She's right, I *am* tired. "How are *you* today, Bubbe?" I ask. "You look tired, too."

She shifts her eyes for a second, as if to make sure no one else is listening, then leans closer and whispers, "I hope God comes and gets me soon."

It's so odd for her to talk about God, especially as someone who might show up and lead her out the door, that I pause and lean in closer.

"Well, I think God will come soon. You've lived a long, good life, Bubbe."

"Vat have I done det's good?" She wrinkles her nose.

"Well, you raised five children."

"Hoo!" Her lips purse and her eyes light up. "*I* did *det*? I kent remember."

"Yes, and you did a lot of cooking, cleaning and sewing for your family. You did a good job."

"Me?" She shakes her head. "Naw. Not me, honey."

"Well, what did you do wrong, then?"

"I kent remember."

"What did you do right?"

"I kent remember."

We both laugh and then her eyes become teary.

"Bubbe, are you lonely?"

"Yes, I'm lonely," she says, "but I don't know vat I'm lonely for."

With the decline of memory and other faculties, she's slipping into a new phase—purer, more innocent. Since the caregivers can take care of her routine needs now, they don't need as much help from me on the physical plane. My visits are for another purpose. My poet friend was right. Bubbe *is* giving me something: The chance to witness this last stage, to walk the wobbly road between two worlds with her.

In the night I dream that Bubbe and I sit by the edge of a large hot tub, naked except for towels wrapped around us. Together we step in slowly and sit down, but the water covers Bubbe's head and I don't know what to do. I stare at her face covered by water, realizing she'll die if I don't pull her up. Part of me wants her to die, but I know that I can't let her because it's not time yet. So I pull her up out of the water, and she breathes.

Great grandmother Rose Fremland with
Lena (on right) and two brothers, circa 1899

Great grandparents Rose and Isaac
Fremland, c. 1950

The wedding Lena and Morris,
December 25, 1910

Morris, Sol, Minnie, Merwin, Bernice, and Lena
Kanter (pregnant with Derril), 1927

Bubbe with Bernice and Derril, 1933

Bubbe with Nancy, 1949

Bernice and Debbie, 1951

Bubbe with Nancy, Debbie, JoAnn, 1952

The Gordon sisters, 1959

The wedding David and Debra, 1981

Nancy's story-doll

Bubbe at the nursing home

Debra, David and Charlie

Ari

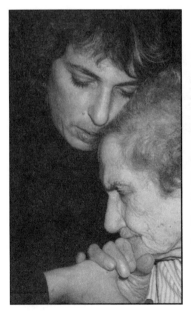

Debra and Bubbe

Rachel and Bubbe

PART III
Home Territory

The named and familiar place here is
Where the young are conceived and birthed,
The living nourished and the ancestors revered.
    —Earth Voices, Robert Beridha

sixteen

January 10

David and I planned a five-day getaway to the Oregon coast this week, but had to cancel it because of the flood. Instead we're heading to a mountain inn, an hour away, to steal twenty-four hours for ourselves.

We check in, then go straight out to the trail where I cross-country ski as David snowshoes alongside. He can't seem to glide on any kind of skis no matter how smooth the terrain, but he trudges along good-naturedly. Afterwards we soak in the outdoor hot tub and breathe in the icy, sharp air as we gaze at Mount Shasta and Mount McLaughlin. Out here there's no Bubbe, just the pulse of our bodies in rhythm, as if our hearts beat in soft unison under the water, tuned to each other.

⌒

Sixteen years ago when we took off on our honeymoon to Hawaii we carried a lot of baggage. Not suitcases—emotional baggage. Three days before the wedding David brought me to his lawyer's office to sign a pre-nuptial agreement. His first marriage had ended after a few years, and in case ours failed he wanted to be sure he kept the house he owned. I was crushed, but I went ahead with the wedding on blind faith.

When we stepped off the plane in Kauai, the warm breeze was so playful and erotic that I put aside the baggage and inhaled. Then exhaled, softer.

Yes. That afternoon we wandered on a beach where hot water gushed up from crevices, bursting every few minutes like warm body fluids. David picked a blood red flower and braided it into my hair. We had landed in the land of hot love: No broken hearts allowed. The rhythm of the islands enveloped us like a new, soft skin. In the next days we danced in yellow moonlight, crooned with ukuleles, sucked on mangos, made slow love, snorkeled on red reefs, and swam with purple fishes.

On the fifth day we decided to venture deeper into the ocean. Instead of spending months getting certified to scuba dive, in Hawaii tourists can take a two-hour group lesson, and then dive thirty feet under with instructors. We were Island adventurers, drenched in warm passion and smothered in fragrant leis, so we signed up to swim into the underworld.

The first hour of instruction included a comprehensive list of every possible death under the sea. The second hour squeaked with rubber suits, surgical breathing apparatus, and stark fear. In the heavy wetsuit my loose, hula-dancing body became stiff and awkward. My swim fins slapped hard on the training deck, jutting out at sharp angles when I tried to walk. The metal tank strapped to my back was leaden, and the flimsy mouth tube my only lifeline. Place the *rubber nozzle in your mouth and breathe slowly. Do not inhale sharply. In and out slowly, naturally.* I envisioned myself at the bottom of the ocean, unable to breathe, the tube floating out of my reach. *Place the mask over your eyes and push firmly to seal. If your vision clouds, tip your head back slightly, and push the seal up and down to let excess water escape.* I imagined my vision clouding as the water rushed into my lungs, my arms flailing, eyes bulging, as I watched one last purple fish float by.

David was grinning as he pulled the apparatus in and out of his mouth, walking easy, tall and lanky in his slick wetsuit—Lloyd Bridges ready for *Sea Hunt.* I breathed into my air hose, *shlshhshhlsh,* and out, *phshhshshhh,* peering closely at the gauge on my tank. *When your gauge goes down to less than one hundred, wave your arms at an instructor. The person whose gauge goes down to one hundred first must signal immediately, and we will all return to the surface.* Breathe in slowly, *shlshhshhls,* breathe out calmly, *phshhshshhh.* I began to shiver uncontrollably.

David slipped off his mask and walked closer. "What's the matter?"

"I'm terrified." The shivers had become spasms; my knees were buckling.

"I thought you wanted to do this." David put his arms around me to steady me, reached behind and loosened my mask, then pulled me over to sit on a bench. "Wasn't this your idea, honey?" He was peering at me curiously, as if he'd never met this quivering creature.

"Yes, I *do* want to do it. I just forgot that I get terrified if I can't breathe."

"Since when?"

"Since this scuba diving lesson."

"Should we forget it, and do something else?"

"NO! After all the time to put on this stuff, I want to at least enjoy the view under the water."

A few minutes later I steeled myself as we plunged into the water. My eyes glared frozen from behind my mask, while bubbles drifted up with each breath: in *shlshlshsh*, out *phshshshsh*, bubble, bubble; in *shlshlshh*, out *phsshshsh*, bubble, bubble. I tried to swim, but I couldn't get my legs to unfurl. My arms flapped at my sides, like turtle fins. The instructor floated by me, gesturing. She pointed to my curled knees, then to her own legs, which she waved in an exaggerated mermaid swish. I tried a swish or two, then snapped back to fetal position. Breathe in *shslshshlsh*, breathe out, *pshshhshsh*, bubble, bubble.

David was somewhere in the drift of divers floating in strange, ghostly bubbles. I searched for his face behind the masks, but my own mask was beginning to get cloudy. *If your vision clouds, tip your head back slightly, and push the seal up and down to let excess water escape.* I tipped my head back, then pushed the seal up and down as carefully as I could. When the mask filled with saltwater, I panicked. Though I waved my arms wildly to get an instructor's attention, no one came, so I headed for the surface, alone. Push up, breathe in, *shlshhshshh*, push harder, kick, breathe out, *phshshshsh*, reach up, splash out.

When I surfaced I pulled the mask off my face and blinked. With one hand I rubbed my eyes while the other hand let go of the mask, which drifted slowly to the bottom, as I tread water to stay afloat. The shore looked a long way off.

An instructor splashed up next to me. "What's going on?"

"My mask was filling with water and I couldn't clear it." My voice sounded hollow and gurgly, as if filled with bubbles and salt.

"Where *is* your mask?"

"I think I dropped it."

She nodded, and for a long moment we tread water.

"Okay," she said, "I'll go down for it. You stay right here."

You can think about a lot of things when you're treading water in the middle of the ocean, like how far away the dock is, or whether your mask will ever be found, or how long you can tread water, or whether a shark could bite your legs off, or if a fish could carry your mask home to his fish family, or where is your husband, and what could he be thinking when he doesn't see you on the bottom of the ocean.

The instructor burst up, waving the mask above her head. She helped me to seal it carefully around my face. "Don't wiggle it. Just leave it on," she warned. Then she took my hand and led me firmly back underwater.

In the eerie slanted sunlight I made out David's long, thin shape apart from the other divers. He looked lost, darting around, swimming in half-circles. When he saw us coming, he swam up, his eyes bulging behind his mask. The instructor pointed to my hand, then to David's, and placed my hand carefully in his. She pointed to both our hands, then clasped her own hands together and waved them in front of David's face. *Hold on to her.*

David nodded and signaled thumbs-up with his free hand. He would not let go. He held my hand so firmly, in fact, that I let my legs uncurl just a little, trying a mermaid swish here and there, swimming next to him, holding on. David pointed to his chest, then his air hose, and back to me. He breathed in, *shlshlshsh,* and I matched his breathing, then out, slowly, *pshshshsh;* we breathed together. He nodded and we swam off, a two-head-ed mermaid, breathing in rhythm. David pointed out a neon parrotfish, then he led me to a little cave and showed me a glowing eel under a rock. *Breathe in, together, breathe out. Swish fins.* It *was* kind of glorious deep under the sea.

When we emerged, the light was fading, but the air still warm and fragrant. After peeling off our wetsuits, we sat on a bench, leaning into each other, grinning. The instructor walked over to check on me. "Diving is scarier for women," she said. I looked puzzled. "Because we bear children," she explained.

Rachel was born nine months later. Six months into the pregnancy, when she was kicking furiously, I sat David down and placed his hand on my stomach. We sat in silence for a few moments. Finally I said, "I'm having our child and I need you to put my name on the deed to our home." Three days later a new deed was issued, and the pre-nuptial agreement torn up. Sixteen years later we swim along, drift apart, surface, then dive deeper. We're still holding hands.

Driving back from Mount Ashland, I lean back, listening to a soft hum at my center, my own motor purring. David holds my hand and says, "Let's make love again when we get home."

"What about the crowd? I ask. "There's Bubbe, Marilyn, and who knows who else today." David shrugs, but keeps stroking my hand. We had to go to the top of a mountain to find a place to be together. Our own house has Bubbe at dead center, with my radar tuned to making her feel at home, aiming her gently towards death.

I ignore her for a few minutes as I unpack, but when I hear voices drifting up from her room, I'm pulled downstairs. Bubbe sits, shaking her head very slowly, like she's trying to comprehend something puzzling. When I sit down, she rubs my hand harder than usual, peers at it, turns it over, as if looking for an answer.

She begins to talk about her house in Russia again, then about her house in North Hollywood. I listen and nod, my mind still distant. Bubbe stops talking in mid-sentence, gazes around, then leans close. "But, vere do I live *now?*"

I answer slowly, deliberately. "This is my house, Bubbe, in Oregon. You live here with us, in your own room." She squinches her eyebrows, looks at me a little suspiciously, then glances over at Marilyn, who sits on a chair by the window, reading a magazine.

"David and I and the kids live upstairs and Marilyn and Rene and Karen stay down here with you so you won't be alone." Bubbe's fingers grip tightly around my wrist as she lets out a long sigh. "Vat vill happen to me naw?"

"I don't know exactly, but I'm always here."

She reaches her hand to the small of her back, shifts her weight and winces. Marilyn has given her liquid Tylenol with codeine, but it doesn't erase all the pain. When she groans I feel powerless. "What can I do for you, Bubbe? I wish I could do more."

She stares at me. "You being vit me means a lot, it means so much, honey. You don't know haw much it means to me."

seventeen

When Bubbe winces in pain, I picture the tumor pressing against her chest, slowly claiming the space between her ribs. Marilyn asked me today if Bubbe knew about the tumor. Even though she saw the x-ray a few years ago, she's probably forgotten, so I decide to tell her again, to help her make sense of her pain.

She looks bewildered, as if I've just delivered a low, blunt blow. "Bed news," she repeats as she shakes her head. "Vat's in de x-rays?"

"A tumor, Bubbe, in your lung."

"Is it kenser?"

"I don't know. It's just a tumor, and it's spreading."

"Nuttin' dey can do?"

"No. That's why your chest and back hurt so much."

She hangs her head. "I got bed news today."

She wants to inform her family, but not the living family—she wants to tell her parents. When I remind her they've been dead for fifty years, she gapes at me. It seems I'm the purveyor of lots of "bed news" today. We go over her entire family, sisters and brothers, which ones are alive, which are dead. She listens intently, nodding and blinking, as if rearranging an old photo album in her mind. Then she grasps my hand.

"Vat's going to happen to me naw?"

"You'll stay here with me and David and the kids and Marilyn, and we'll take care of you."

"Dey can't do nuttin' about da tumer?"

I imagine the tumor spreading, as her body crumbles around it in soft collapse. I shake my head. "Nothing."

"Vere vill I go?"

"To heaven, I think."

She leans closer and whispers, "Not me. I'll go to hell."

I glance up to see Ari and his friend Matt tiptoeing into the room. They must want something important, because Ari still avoids coming downstairs for any reason. From the minute Bubbe arrived, when his big concern was, "Do I have to kiss her?" he's kept his distance. When I tell them that Bubbe and I are in the middle of an important conversation, they sit down quietly, listening while we talk about death. It's odd to see these two soccer buddies who are always running on the field or zooming on their skateboards sit stock-still, as if someone just pressed the slo-mo button on their lives.

When we're done, I point Ari out to Bubbe, to reorient her to the present. "This is your GREAT-GRANDSON, ARI," I say loudly, gesturing at him.

"I know dat," she says. "Of course I know him." When he gets up, I tell him to say goodbye.

"GOODBYE, BUBBE!"

She eyes him, puckers her face and says, "Haw 'bout a nice kiss?" He leans over and kisses her solemnly on the cheek. His face is bright red.

"Goodbye, Tommy," she chirps.

Bubbe sleeps most of the next day, then says nothing about the tumor, so we don't bring it up. David is leading Shabbat services and Ari is at a friend's house, so Rachel, her friend Nicole, and I order Thai food for dinner to eat downstairs with Karen and Bubbe. She's in good spirits, refueled by her day of sleep, and when the girls walk in with the candles she sits up and announces, "Vell, look who came to see me!"

We sing Shabbat songs while Bubbe croons and claps along. "Shabbat Shalom!" She cocks her head to one side, slaps her hands together, and grins, toothless. "Shabbat Shalom!" When we light the candles she rattles off the *Bracha*, then tears off chunks of challah with her wobbly, thick fingers and stuffs them into her mouth. She even tastes the wine, and the girls giggle as she reaches to take more slurps. She likes the Thai noodles and chicken, but spits the eggplant into her napkin.

"Do you remember what foods you used to cook for Shabbat dinner, Bubbe?" Karen asks.

"Vell," Bubbe sits back, thinking. "I'd make a chicken vit rice pudding, and a carrot ring, and den a date cake for da dessert." She leans close, as if confiding a secret. "You couldn't cook eny sour cream vit da chicken because you hed to keep *milchedik*, de dairy, separate from *fleishedik*, de meat." The girls huddle in as they ask more questions. Bubbe's face is flushed from the wine; she's on a roll. She describes making *hamantaschen*, the triangle pastry eaten on Purim, demonstrating patting and turning the dough, then checking as we imitate her.

Rachel says, "You'll have to help us make *hamentaschen* on Purim."

"Ven is dat coming?"

"In a couple of months."

Bubbe wags her finger at Rachel. "You gels better prectice. I might be going home before Purim."

After dinner, as Karen tucks her into bed, Bubbe says, "I hed a dream about my parents today. Do you ever dream about people who are dead?"

"Yes, I dream of my grandparents all the time," Karen tells her. Apparently Bubbe remembers, after seeing them in her dream, that her parents are dead. It's as if she tiptoes in and out of another realm, peering ahead to get ready for her passage.

⁓

November 1988

We've been sitting at Bubbe's table videotaping for an hour, and she's still going strong. "How did you meet Grandpa?" I ask her.

"Vell, I vanted to get married to get away from my modder, but it vas hard to meet anyvon, because I couldn't go anyvere. A frend of mine told her brodder dat I vould make a good vife, because I did all da houseverk, see. So vun day she decided to bring him over to meet me. She said, 'You'll see her at home, you'll see vat a *balabusta* she is.'"

I try to imagine my grandmother, young and slim, greeting a young man, her only suitor. In my mind she pauses in a whirlwind of pots and dust and kids, then takes in a deep breath before she sees her future, my grandfather, at the door.

"Oy, honey, I looked terrible. I hed on an old housedress, my hair vas a mess, but I guess he liked me. So he'd come around sometimes, and ve'd go for a valk or go out a little bit if my modder vasn't home."

"Did you like him right away?"

"I liked him, he vas polite, he vas a hendsome man. He vas twenty-five-years old and he vas verking already as a tailor. He tot da vorld of my modder. His modder had died, see, ven he vas two years old. Vell, he put my modder up on a pedastal, like she vas a kveen." Grandma rolls her eyes and I widen mine in imitation. We both know her mother didn't belong on any pedestal.

"How long before you got married?"

"It vas just a few monts, maybe, ven he came to my modder and said he vanted to make a vedding. I'll never forget vat she said to him. She said, 'So, you vant to make a vedding for a dollar or a hundred dollars?' I vas so ashamed, honey. Dis is how much she velued me, her dodder. For a dollar, or a hundred dollars?" Bubbe lowers her eyes and stares at her fingers. For a moment I close my eyes so I won't see the shame in her face.

"But Morris told her he'd pay for da vedding, so she could buy vatever she needed and charge it to him. Vell, my modder vent and everyvere she went, she got more den she needed. So if she needed a pound of butter, she'd order two or tree pounds and charge it to Morris. If she needed two yards of febric, she'd order four because he vas paying for it. So he kem to me and said, 'Your modder is taking edvantage; she's taking more den she needs. I just vanted you should hear it from me.' She vas stealing from my husband and everyvun in all da stores knew about it. I vas so ashamed, but Morris never said anyting to her. He idolized her."

This is a twist in her story that I never knew, that her husband adored the mother who abused her. Grandma sits, nodding, and I nod with her, our bodies tipping a little. David glances up from the camcorder at the two of us rocking in unison.

Finally I ask, "You got pregnant right after that, right?"

"I vas seventeen ven I got married, on Christmas day, 1910. Minnie vas born on my eighteent birtday, about nine monts later. A veek after I hed Minnie, my modder had a beckache so she hed to stay in bed." She grimaces as she holds her back in mock pain, and I know what's coming.

"I had to go and take care of my younger sisters and do all of da houseverk for her. I had a veek-old baby, I vas exhausted, honey, but vat could I do? I tink my modder got sick on purpose, so I'd come back and do all of da verk.

"Sol vas born ven Minnie vas eighteen monts old, so I didn't hev any break. Ven I come home from da hospital vit Sol, Minnie vas jealous. Ve had a cradle hanging up in da room and she vanted me to rock her in da cradle. All night long I vas up, nursing da new baby, and rocking Minnie. In da morning, I vas so tired, I took a stick and I smashed dat cradle."

She raises her hand to flail an imaginary stick as she speaks. She's an old woman, ninety-five, sitting at a table, but as she strikes, I lean back a little, startled. There's something in the set of her jaw, the flash of her eye, that I've seen on my mother's face.

She lowers her arm and looks at me again. "I smashed it to bits. I'm not proud of it honey, but det's vat I did." She has told me this story before and will tell it many times again before she is too old to remember it, repeating it as if to purge it, pick a scab off a sore, reach for forgiveness.

"You know, Minnie and I, ve don't get along so good, even now. She's seventy-seven years old, but dey say dat sometimes tings from your childhood ken affect you later. I told her I vas sorry if I'd done tings to hurt her. She says she don't remember."

⌒

Today when I go downstairs Bubbe starts talking right away, as if we were continuing a conversation from a few seconds ago. She squeezes my hand and says, "You know, I ran into somebody yesterday who knew me in da old country and she told me my parents died. I didn't know dat." She shakes her head. "It's like a dream. It's as if I could see my house dere."

I listen, stroke her shoulder, wait for more.

"I vas sorry to hear about my fadder," she says. "He vas a vonderful man."

"What about your mother?"

"She vas a fine voman."

I hesitate, trying to make sense of this. "Maybe you're ready to forgive your mother now?"

"For vat?"

"Well, she wasn't always good to you."

She stares back at me like I'm crazy.

"Well, what about when you had to take care of your baby brother when you were only seven? You put him down for a minute and he fell down the stairs in the windmill. Do you remember that day, Bubbe?" She's told me so many times how her mother beat her for letting her brother fall that I imagine the image must be etched in her psyche.

She gazes at me vacantly and waves her hands in front of her face, as if swatting away a fly. "I don't know vat you're talking about, honey."

eighteen

On Shabbat, we stand in a semi-circle around Bubbe's bed and light the candles as she says the *Bracha* softly. It's as if the flames transport her back from her dreams of the old country, and she's right here, focused and calm. Before David goes out to lead services, he says, "Why don't you bring Bubbe? There won't be many more chances for her to come."

"Bubbe, do you want to go to services with us?" I ask.

"I'd love to," she answers.

Karen quickly feeds Bubbe dinner while Rachel scrambles through the closet to pick out something for her to wear. As soon as she's dressed, she says, "Me—going to services?" She puts a look of mock horror on her face. "Naw! Dey'll kick me out!"

"No they won't," I tell her. "Everyone will be honored that you're there."

"Vhy?"

"Because you're one hundred and three and you're my bubbe."

"No, dey'll kick me out."

"No way," I tell her firmly, "I'm the *rebbitzen*, and you're my bubbe, and if *I* say you can go, then you can go." She shrugs.

I call Sue, who drives a van with a lift, to pick us up on her way to services, but it's a half-hour before she arrives. Bubbe looks confused and small sitting in her wheelchair all dressed up with nowhere to go. She's wrapped in her blue wool coat with a big fur collar that must have been expensive and stylish in the '40s. Now her shriveled face with its sunken jaw looks lost and mismatched peering out of that lush, furry frame.

When we finally get her on the lift to the van, her eyes bulge as she grips the wheelchair arms. One fall and I can see the brittle bones in her body shattering on our cement driveway. She's so frail, hanging on between life and death, that seeing her suspended on the lift just accentuates her precarious position.

As we enter the social hall in the church that we rent for services, David announces, "Debbie's 103-year-old grandmother is entering. Please rise for Bubbe." I push her slowly down the aisle as David strums a melody on the guitar. The congregation hums and gazes at Bubbe as if she were a bride.

"BUBBE!" I yell in her ear, "They're all standing for you!"

"Vat for?"

"You're the oldest member of the congregation. You're the Bubbe!"

I wheel her up to the candles and take her hand so that we can light the Shabbat candles together and say the *Bracha*. She glances at the crowd and says, "I forgot it." I lean down to remind her until she recites in her thick accent, "*Bruchatoi adonoi, Eloheinu, melechoilom . . .*" The group is quiet, as if the entire room has taken in a breath. An elderly man comes over, kneels down next to Bubbe and begins to talk to her in Yiddish. She can't hear, blinks back and says, "Git haim."

"She wants to go home," he translates.

After the candle lighting, Bubbe sits, shifting about in her scratchy wool coat. When I reach over to try to take it off, she shouts, "NO!" and clutches it as if I'm about to strip her naked. She wants to look proper in Synagogue. As the service goes on, she squirms, then dozes on and off. Someone gets up and tells a long story. Bubbe leans over to me. "I'm sick," she says.

I whisper loudly in her ear, "Do you want to go home now?"

She stares at me and hollers, "DA SERVICE ISN'T OVER! YOU KENT LEAVE IN DE MIDDEL!" Her timing is perfect, right in a dead pause, so her words ring out through the whole congregation.

Afterward, Karen rides home with Bubbe, who falls into a deep sleep. In the morning she doesn't remember going anywhere, but Karen tells her everyone prayed with her and she likes hearing this.

That night I dream that Bubbe insists on going out walking, so we bundle up, and I scurry along as she charges ahead without her walker. A man with long white hair on a red motorcycle pulls up and she hops on. They ride off, speeding around in circles, laughing. When I realize they've vanished, I begin to worry. What if something happens to her? I go to the police, but no one will do anything. I think, "What will I tell all the relatives?" I decide to go door to door to ask if anyone has seen Bubbe and the motorcycle man, but I wake without having found her.

When I tell Bubbe about my dream the next morning she laughs. "Did you ever ride on a motorcycle?" I ask her.

"No, I don't tink so." We talk about all the things she has ridden in: a car, a bus, a train, an airplane, a horse and buggy, and a boat to America.

When I remind her about our trip to the synagogue, she says, "Dey all stood up for me? Vhy?"

"Because you're the oldest and the wisest. You're the Bubbe. They were honored to be in your presence." She shakes her head in disbelief, but then holds her neck up a little, as if preening in a mirror. She enjoys hearing this so much that I repeat it to her many times in the next weeks.

Bubbe falls into a deep sleep for the rest of the weekend, waking rarely and hardly eating. When awake, she repeats to Karen, "I'm sick."

When Marilyn arrives Sunday night, Bubbe sits up slowly and stares. "Who's dying?" she asks.

Marilyn tells her, "Bubbe's dying."

"Bubbe's dying."

"But," Marilyn says, "her soul will live on."

nineteen

Monday morning Bubbe looks up and asks me, "Vere's the rest of my femmily?" We go over the roster of who is left one more time. Bubbe taps her finger in the air, as if marking off an invisible slate.

"My sister Sadie, she lives in Minnesota; my brodder Joe is still around, but he don't remember tings anymore."

"Don't forget your daughters, Derril and Minnie," I remind her.

She frowns, pauses, then tallies them among the living. "I still kent believe my perents are gone."

"Bubbe," I ask her, "Do you think that when you die you might see the people who've died before you?"

"No, haw could you see anyvun who's dead?"

"Well, some people think that when you die you go someplace like heaven, and you can see people you love who've died."

"I don't tink so."

"Well, I hope I'll see my mother again because I miss her so much." I find myself getting teary as I tell her this, though I haven't cried over missing my mother in years. Talking to Bubbe, though, I feel like she's in the next room, and I ache to touch her.

❧

Since it was my mother's dream to live near the ocean, as soon as the last of their children left home, my parents moved out of the suburbs, to Venice

Beach. She and Milt could stroll the boardwalk together and breathe cool salt air amid street vendors, body builders, and funky delicatessens. No more teenagers, no lawns to water, no orthodontists or child psychiatrists.

Each time they drove home to their new building, my mother waited until they rounded the corner onto Pacific Avenue. "That's my favorite view," she'd say, "when you can first see the ocean." The streets were full of gas stations, telephone poles, freeway noise, and rubbish. But turn the corner and there, flanked by palms, she'd see a picture-postcard glimpse of the ocean: a rising band of pale sand, a stripe of turquoise, then the expanse of sky.

In 1974, a year and a half after their move, she had surgery for tumors and adhesions, and pains that wouldn't go away. When the surgeon came to find us in the waiting room, he said, "We opened her up, and she was so full of cancer, we just closed her back up."

In the sunlight of her bedroom two weeks after the surgery her skin is pale, her cheeks sunken. For many years her face was round and flushed, but now she's so thin that her teeth protrude, as if they're ill-fitting dentures. She runs her tongue over them, turns her head on her pillow, and stares at the wall of mirrored doors across from her.

She's decided to try chemotherapy even though it offers little hope. The doses come in small glass vials that the home-health nurse injects twice daily. The toxins wreck her bowels so she has to drag her body to the toilet over and over, to expel puddles of gray, reeking fluid. My father and I wipe it off the floor, off the sheets, always flushing, swabbing, behind her. After a week, we discontinue the chemical, which is called "5-F-U." "Five Fuck-You," my mother calls it. When we tell the home-health nurse this, she laughs. "Your mother has spirit," she says. But I see her spirit leaking away, as if we scoop it off the floor with her pools of poisoned fluid, and watch it spiral down the drain.

"Sit down," my mother says to me, "you're tired." She pats the bed next to her. At twenty-three I've come back from college in Oregon to be with my mother before she dies.

"No, I'm fine," I say, but I sit down anyway, dangling my sandals over the bedside.

"Take your shoes off. Lie down." My mother scoots over with effort, her body a heavy, limp sack.

I slip my sandals off slowly. They're full of scratchy sand from my walk on the beach that morning. I lie down next to her, but keep my head off the pillow.

"You know, Debbie," she says, "Of all my children, you are the one that has always been a joy to me. A free spirit."

I stare. Not one cell in my body feels free. I feel like I'm drowning in her death, slipping into emptiness. What I can't see then is how much of myself I've poured into trying to be a joy to her, striving to shore up her picture of the family, being the perfect daughter. I don't feel my own spirit, only the weight of her need, and the pull of her death.

I will go on searching for a different kind of mother for years without knowing it. I will tell stories of strong women, pull talking dolls and magic rings from my pocket, groping for traces of guidance, wisps of mothering. I will even bring my grandmother home to live with me, fumbling to unravel the umbilical chord. But I will never be able to fix anything for my mother, or she for me. I want to shout at her *I'm not free at all! Can't you see that?* Instead I nod silently as if I agree and squeeze her hand, because I know this is what she wants.

"Here. Look out the window from here." My mother points ahead and I see through the window above the dresser, beyond a row of grimy concrete buildings, past a bent palm, the ocean. A strip of pale sand, a band of dazzling turquoise, then the wash of sky, forever.

⌒∽

Wednesday morning, I wander in the kitchen before work, foggy-headed, making coffee, when Marilyn knocks on the kitchen door. Rene is about to relieve her for her mid-week day off, and she wants to talk before she leaves her shift. "Of course," David says as he leads her to the kitchen table. I glance at the coffeepot, but it's not ready yet.

"Here," says Marilyn, as she hands me a long list of written complaints: The kitchen faucet drips, the new bed we bought her is too soft and the frame creaks, the stove is hard to light, she wants us to buy only organic vegetables for her, and when the other caregivers miss medications, she doesn't know what to do. I nod my head dumbly as I stare at the list.

"If Karen doesn't give Bubbe a pill on time, then I don't know if I'm supposed to give her the dose or wait 'til the next time."

I try to explain the possible options carefully but she keeps interrupting. "Marilyn," I say sharply, "let me finish my sentence."

When we're done she asks, "Are you mad at me?"

"No," I say, "not at all. It's just hard for me to deal with so many things at once." As he leads her out the door, David assures Marilyn that it's wonderful that she brings us feedback so we can help solve the problems. Afterwards he tells me I was rude.

"But it's morning," I plead, "and I haven't even had my coffee."

"You're bigger than that," he says. "Have some compassion."

"No coffee, no compassion," I say, but I know he's right. David is always kind and patient with Marilyn, but he doesn't spend nearly as much time with her and Bubbe as I do. He can be empathetic, yet detached. Unlike him, I let everyone and everything burrow under my skin, Bubbe and Marilyn included. It may make me grouchy, but it is precisely because I allow her under my skin, I realize, that I'm able to enter Bubbe's world. I wish I had a one-way valve around my heart that would open enough to allow me to visit Bubbe's dreams, smell her dusty cheeks, follow the tide of her memories, then snap shut so I could handle the outside world with tact.

twenty

In his sermon last Friday night David talked again about how holy it is to be with Bubbe—how sharp she is, and how she can still raise or demote him with one word, "Dere's the rabbi," or, "He's supposed to be the rabbi," depending on if she approves of his behavior.

I disapprove of his behavior. Today is Thursday and he hasn't seen her since last Friday. I know he resents it if I nag him, but I'm sick of him sermonizing about how holy it is to be in her presence when he doesn't make time to visit her. At services a middle-aged man with a Guatemalan poncho and a braided yarmulke walked up to the microphone and announced, "I want everyone to know how wonderful it is that David is doing this for his mother."

"It's my grandma," I corrected him, sharply.

"Well, what he's done for his relative."

"David's not related to her," I declared, and was instantly embarrassed for sounding so small and selfish.

David is getting ready to go to lead services in Central Oregon this weekend. Since his job here is part-time, he travels once a month to make ends meet. As he folds his white shirts and prayer shawl carefully into the suitcase, I decide it's time to speak up. "You're running around serving other people, but you're avoiding the *mitzvah* right here in your house."

David glances at his suitcase. "What are you talking about?"

"You think you're so holy, but you can't handle doing something simple. You tell me how meaningful it is to sit on the deathbed of a congregant's mother, sharing the profound moments with the family, but you don't sit on the deathbed at home." I'm pretty sure now that I'm morally superior to him and even if he gets angry and defensive, it will be worth it. I'm on a roll.

"You tell stories of how bonded you were with a girl with a brain tumor, how she played a tape of you singing that echoed through the halls of the hospital—but you don't bond with Bubbe, because it doesn't serve your ego."

I steel myself for a counter-attack, but David just sits down on the bed and shakes his head. "I know," he says. "It's true. I don't know why, but the more intense part of life is what I'm good at. The day-to-day stuff is harder for me."

I was expecting him to at least be chagrinned. *Isn't this the part in the Hasidic stories where the Holy Man learns his lesson about the True Hidden Mitzvahs in life, begs for forgiveness and transforms by having his Soul exposed and broken?* But David stares soberly and nods. "Maybe that's why I can be a rabbi," he says. "I can tolerate intensity, be there at the deep moments. That's where I'm comfortable."

His quiet response has stemmed my attack, so I tell him what I really want is more support. "I don't know if it matters to Bubbe if you visit, but it makes *me* feel better."

A part of me is simply scared. *When I'm too old or sick to call for your attention, will you pass me by, too?* In my mind I hear Paul Simon crooning, *Why can't you love me for who I am, where I am?* The answer is, *Cause that's not the way that love is, baby. This is how I love you.* This is how David loves me, by listening and trying to give what he can. This is how I love him, by accepting that. But I know there's a soft, empty tunnel in my chest that he can't fill. If I listen closely I can always hear something stretching in there, scurrying about, aching to be soothed.

He puts his arm around my shoulder and we sit, dangling our legs over the side of the bed. "I'll try harder," he says.

The next day I'm tired all day, feeling as if I'm hauling around an old, dull sadness. The longer Bubbe is here, the more I sense it's connected to her, like a rope with a leaden anchor that binds us together and keeps us from floating free.

Bubbe sits. She swings her feet, waves her hand in the air, fumbles for her dreidle, and spins. She says, "dreidle, dreidle, dreidle," with a bewildered, half-smile. She's always glad to see me, but mostly she sits, not sure what to do—more lost, more tired, bored and lonely. She goes to bed, gets out of bed, spins the dreidle, eats, goes back to bed, gets up, spins and mumbles, "dreidle, dreidle, dreidle."

I look down at my hands and I see Bubbe's hands, waving, reaching, stroking. Today mine seem as empty as hers. Open, useless, not knowing what to reach for.

When David returns on Sunday night, I feel a little better, but when we settle into bed my sleep is fitful. I wake at two a.m. and sit up in bed. "Senna Tea!" I say out loud.

David rolls over and stares at me. "Sanity?"

"No! Senna tea! It's an herbal remedy we can try for Bubbe's constipation."

"Mmm. . ." David turns and goes right back to sleep, snoring within seconds. He does that so easily that it annoys me every time.

When I get up to go to the bathroom, I hear Rachel crying, so I pad across the hall to her room, and open the door. The dim light of her bedside lamp gives off an other-worldly glow. The room is a montage of teenage things—beaded jewelry, a stereo with outsized speakers, shelves full of women's fiction, Barbara Kingsolver next to Terry Tempest Williams, open journals where she writes and draws, textbooks strewn about, and a calendar marked with all her events in neon colors. Still, she has a teddy bear and her stuffed bunny in bed with her. Young woman in transition.

"What's wrong?" I sit down on her bed.

"Ev-er-y-thing." The sobbing increases.

I reach over and rub her shoulders. "Tell me."

"Dad didn't give me the driving lesson he promised today 'cause he didn't get home till after dark. He wants to do it tomorrow, but I can't. It always has to be on his terms. I hate Dad."

I nod and keep rubbing. "What else?

"My French teacher hates me. You can tell because she only calls on me when she knows I don't know the answer. She picks on me."

I groan with her. "And?"

"And I can't finish my paper for English because I have rehearsals for theatre group every day and I have mid-terms next week and I know I'm going to fail them all."

I keep stroking.

"It's all too much!" she wails. "I just can't do it all!"

I lie down next to her. "Tell the negative voices shut up. You don't have to get all A's, and you don't have to go to every rehearsal. It will all sort itself out."

"I'm just going to fail everything." Rachel snuggles up next to me.

"You can't fail everything. You're doing your best and you don't have to be perfect."

I have an eerie feeling I've snatched this speech from the lines I tell myself. My daughter is an excellent student of me. Perfectionist, take care of everything and everybody. Overachievers Anonymous.

In high school when things got too difficult for me, I started smoking pot and failing classes rather than handle the weight of the pressure on my chest. I didn't ask my mother for help, since I was pretending to be competent for her, and by the time I was fifteen, I pretended I didn't care. With every puff, the pressure got lighter.

Now I feel like I'm watching a rerun movie of myself. Rachel may have adopted my perfectionism as if I handed her a treadmill to run on, but maybe the mother in this movie can listen to her daughter so she doesn't have to pretend to be fine. Maybe that's the best *I* can do. I put my hand on her heart. "I'm filling up your tank with love," I tell her. It's a game we've played since Rachel was little. "Come on, just feel it."

Rachel kisses me. "You can go back to bed now, Mommy," she says.

When I walk downstairs the next morning Bubbe wakes and calls out, "Vere's Debbie?" I sit down while she squints and blinks at me. Marilyn hands me a warm washcloth, so I gently wipe her cheeks and dab at her crusty eyes. She calls to Marilyn, "Vere's my vater?"

She waits for Marilyn to go, then says in a loud whisper, "I HOPE she'll get it for me." Marilyn brings a glass of "vater," the usual mixture of prune and apple juices. Bubbe sips it, then begins to speak to me in Yiddish. I nod, though I don't understand a word. She's like a child just awakened from a nap, confused, tousled and smiling in her flowered nightgown. Her odor is sour and rotting, but her feel is pure innocence.

She stops the Yiddish in mid-sentence, stares at me and announces, "You're Bubbe."

I shake my head, "No, you're Bubbe. I'm Debbie"

"I'm Deb-bie." She nods and smiles.

"No, *I'm* Debbie."

We giggle as she gives me a loud sucking kiss on my cheek, then strains to focus on me, inches from her face. "You stay here, don't go avay," she says. I want to pull back from her gaze, widen the focus so I can tell who's who, but I feel her gnarled grasp and breathe in the scent of her slack skin.

"Don't worry, Bubbe," I tell her, "I'm not going anywhere."

twenty-one

"It's January 30 today," I tell Bubbe. "Nancy's birthday." She gives me a blank stare. What I don't say is it's also the ten-year anniversary, the *yortzeit,* of my father's death. Miltie would always call on our birthdays, so when there was no phone call on her thirty-ninth birthday, my sister Nancy knew something was wrong. He was only sixty-eight, but he was depressed and his heart was failing. "Maybe he went out of town," I told her, but something made us both uneasy. Four days later, when he hadn't returned calls, we had the police break down his door to find Miltie's body, dark and bloated, on his bed. The apartment reeked for weeks, even after we dragged out the mattress, opened the windows to let in the sea air, and pulled up the carpet.

"*Nancy's forty nine today,*" I say it louder, trying to engage Bubbe.

She stares harder at me. "I'm not special," she says.

"Did you ever feel special when you were younger?

"No, I never vas special to anyvone."

I pull out a photo album and point to pictures of Bubbe with my sisters, cousins, and me. "You were special to your grandchildren."

She shrugs. "Naw, I vasn't."

The page is open to a picture of Nancy, three years old, standing on a chair in a puffy-sleeved pinafore, with Bubbe next to her, smiling. "There's Nancy with you when she was little, Bubbe."

Bubbe runs her fingers over Nancy's face. "She looks like a little doll." As I turn the page a handmade piece of paper drops into Bubbe's lap. It has dried flowers pressed into a deep soft pink, like the lining of a shell. Words float through the colors, *To Grandma, Love, Nancy.*

"Look Bubbe, you saved this card that Nancy made."

She rubs the flowers slowly as if she's reading Braille. "Det Nency," she says. "She hes Golden Hands."

A year ago Nancy phoned from San Diego and told me she was taking a Book Arts class. "What are you working on?" Nancy's specialty has always been ceramics, but she's good in any medium. I pictured a specially bound book made with handmade paper and swirling colors. A Nancy creation.

"My book is a doll."

"How can a book be a doll?"

"I made her out of bits of fabric from my past and she has little books and scrolls coming out of parts of her."

"What are the books and scrolls about?"

"Incest."

I drew in my breath. For a few years Nancy's been talking about how our Uncle Bernie molested her. She recovered the memories in therapy. I remember that Uncle Bernie would tickle us and my father told him to stop. I didn't know that Bernie did more than tickle Nancy

Last year Nancy said she remembers our sister JoAnn molesting her. *How could this be true?* I know JoAnn was cruel to Nancy, tormenting her when they were little. Even now they don't speak to each other. But a sister *sexually molesting* another sister? *This cannot be my family.*

Nancy described the doll, but I couldn't listen. I tidied the books on my table with one hand, twirled the phone cord with the other, thought about what to make for dinner. *Nancy says JoAnn tortured her with live goldfish, making her swallow them, and sticking them in her vagina.* I pushed it to the corners of my mind.

"I want you to see my doll," she said. "It's going to be in a show in a gallery here."

In a public gallery? "Well, if can't make it to this show, maybe I'll get to see it another time."

I didn't go to that gallery, but the doll was featured in other shows. Nancy sent me a clipping from the *Chicago Sun-Times*.

Nancy Gordon's 'Story Doll' . . . is a simple enough object, something you could find in a craft store, perhaps sewn by someone's grandmother. But the little books and scrolls and handwritten notes flowing out of its pockets and tied to its skirt by colorful strings tell horrific stories of childhood abuse and violence. These are familiar enough stories but their association with such a feminine and childlike object illustrates them in a particularly dramatic fashion.

Six months later Rachel, her friend Kirsten, and I visited San Diego. We went to the beach, shopped in Tijuana, rented girl videos, and watched them on Nancy's tiny TV. Her house is not the kind where you'd expect to find a TV. The walls and shelves are adorned with artwork, sculpture, and ethnic crafts. Each space is arranged as a creation in itself.

On the second night Nancy sat us down in a small circle on the living room rug to present her doll. She unpacked it slowly from a special crate. Her hair was woven with flowers and strands of yarn, her mouth zipped shut with a plastic zipper. Out of her heart tumbled a scroll of words, out of her crotch an accordion of paper. She sat on Nancy's lap, another entity in the room, patched together, broken and whole.

The scrolls of words were mixed with photos from our childhood. One photo near the heart showed JoAnn, Nancy, and me lined up on the sidewalk in front of our grandmother's house, squinting in the San Fernando Valley sun. The scroll read: *Bubbe made carrot ring, scrambled eggs flopsy, and lots of chicken. Don't you girls look just like flowers? she would say.*

A fish was sewn near the crotch and another near the mouth. The belly held a story. *The smaller girl does not move. Her big sister throws a dead angelfish at her. She misses. The little one runs out but her path is blocked. A hand holds a fish to her mouth. Eat it, says her sister . . . or I will put it in another place while you sleep. This has happened before. The little girl eats the fish. In the night she wakes to vomit alone. Close the door, leave no mess. No one must ask about stray fish on the bathroom floor.*

Words crept from the zippered mouth . . . *If you tell I will kill you.*

On another scroll, near the heart, was written, *The two younger sisters settle in with their books. The oldest sister now has a room across the house. The middle sister makes a list of good stories for the little sister to read when she is bigger. When they grow up, the youngest sister is a storyteller.*

We passed the doll around, read her words, examined her secret parts, and stroked her soft body. When I looked up at Rachel and Kirsten I saw their eyes were teary. I struggled for words, then burst into tears. Finally I said to Nancy, "I don't want this to have happened to you." She nodded. Then we all sat, stared at the doll, and cried.

twenty-two

Bubbe opens her eyes this morning to see a heap of letters on her bedside table, strewn with hearts and flowers. "Vat's dis?"

"They're Valentines, just for you, Bubbe!" Marilyn moves in to show her.

Bubbe stares. "Whose det from?" As Marilyn sifts through them, Bubbe comments. "Oh, det's from JoAnn. . . Derril sent dis. . . My sister Sadie." She runs her fingers over the hearts and frills, feels the paper and sighs.

"Look how popular you are!" says Marilyn. "You got more than anyone!"

I hear the edge in Marilyn's voice. *No one's paying attention to my needs, only to Bubbe's.* I should have gotten Marilyn a card, should listen to her more, so she feels valued.

Bubbe shrugs. Her head bobs back and forth, "So, I got lots of cards."

"JoAnn called this morning to see how you're doing," Marilyn tells her.

Bubbe shakes her head. "I hope she's going to be okay dere, in Keneda. De doctor's aren't so good." She looks up at me, eyes narrowed, lips pursed. I haven't seen that look in a long time. The kind of look that's aimed at producing guilt. *Why don't you care more about your sister?*

I do care, I want to tell her, *but I don't know what to do.*

Growing up, JoAnn had creamy skin, shiny curls, and a vixen smile that attracted boys for miles. In the 1960s she'd pay me twenty-five cents to clean up after her when she got ready for a date. I gladly gathered sticky mascara and lipstick tubes, scrubbed the sink, and picked up the cast-off outfits strewn around her room like dead bodies. My beautiful, popular sister.

Now she lives just over the border, in Canada, but I keep my distance. JoAnn can pull me in with charm and guile, then sting with a scorpion's twist. For the last twenty five years she's been in bed with pain that began in her back, then gradually mushroomed through her body, wrecking her health.

Ten years ago, when JoAnn told me she needed to have a hysterectomy because of cervical cancer, I spoke to my father on the phone. He drew in his breath, then spoke in a slow monotone.

"Oh God. Not cancer." I could almost see his face take on the grey shadow that he carried during my mother's illness.

"I'll go," I told him. "I'll take care of her." Ari was only two years old, and it was hard to be away from my kids, but I needed to do this for JoAnn, and even more for my dad.

In the hospital bed her round face was lost in a billowy nest of pillows. Her skin was smooth, her face childlike, as if the flush on her cheeks was excitement, not post-surgical fever. When I bent to kiss her, one of the pillows near her feet dislodged and landed on the ground. I bent to pick it up.

"You'll have to get a new pillowcase!" She was fully awake, even on morphine.

I sat at her bedside, repositioning pillows for four days. When one shifted or dropped on the floor, I rebuilt the configuration carefully. Her skin had to be scrubbed with special cleanser for twenty minutes three times a day, and her toothbrush air-dried, laid at an angle above the sink.

"Otherwise I'll get an infection," she explained.

We waited for the post-surgery pathology report on the cancer, but it never came.

The next week, back in Ashland, I offered to call the doctors myself and get the reports. On the phone, I heard JoAnn sigh. "There is no pathologist report. There was nothing to test."

"What do you mean?"

"Well, it was actually a pre-cancerous condition."

"You mean the surgery was elective?"

There was along silence.

"Why did you lie to me, JoAnn?"

"I wanted you to come."

I thought of my father's face. "Do you know how much dad suffered thinking you had cancer?

"I didn't think of that."

JoAnn hadn't thought of that in 1975 either, when she pulled me outside of my parents' beach apartment a few hours after my mother's funeral. "I did something," she said. I looked at her oddly serene face. Everyone else had been crying for hours.

"What did you do?"

"I took a half a bottle of codeine pills."

I walked with her on the beach as the sun set, feeding her cups of coffee, and hiding her from my father. How could she devastate him more than he already was? Couldn't she put her own pain aside for a few days? But she couldn't.

A year and a half ago, in Seattle for a bar mitzvah, we were just a few hours from Vancouver, and David and the kids had never met my oldest sister. They've talked on the phone and we've sent pictures, but I've stayed away since the hysterectomy, because no one but JoAnn can make me feel sad and angry and confused all at once.

This time I hardly recognized her propped against her pillows on the couch in her tiny apartment. She was plump and doughy, her dark eyes bulging in her pale face. Her smile, an odd frozen grin, showed gaps in her front teeth. She wore an oversized, boxy man's shirt with random buttons missing, as if the buttons, like her teeth, had fallen from disease.

I walked in, urging Rachel and Ari forward. When they bent to kiss her she grabbed them, exclaiming, "You're so big, so beautiful!" To me she said, "You've changed so much! You have gray in your hair and wrinkles!" I realized that since JoAnn hardly goes outside, her skin is pasty and pale, but still smooth.

We pulled our chairs close to the couch to talk. When JoAnn said she uses sign language in her work with the Association for Disabilities, Rachel, who was thirteen, was excited. "How do you sign 'What's for dinner?'" she asked.

"I forgot," JoAnn said. When Rachel asked her to sign another phrase, she shrugged. "I can read it better than I can sign it."

"Okay, what's this?" Rachel signed a sentence she'd learned in school.

JoAnn shifted on her pillows. "I guess you sign it different than we do in Canada. "

Later Rachel asked, "Why does Aunt JoAnn lie?"

"I'm not sure she knows what's real anymore."

In the motel room when the kids were asleep, I fell into bed, weeping. "Look what my sister has become," I moaned to David.

"She's still your sister, David says." She's still in there, I can see it."

I can't see it. I want to hide from her strange, glazed eyes. I want to say, " Push yourself off of those pillows, and be my big sister again!" But I can't stop her disease, physical or mental, any more than I could stop my mother's drinking, or my father's sadness. She's as lost to me as my parents, not dead, but slowly burying herself alive.

The next day JoAnn wanted us to visit the sea wall in Stanley Park, but she wouldn't ride in our Suburu wagon. "It's too small for me," she said. We rented a big sedan, then stuffed pillows into the back seat and crammed two laundry sacks full of extra pillows into the trunk with JoAnn's wheelchair.

I sat in the backseat with JoAnn, who lay down and plopped her feet in my lap. She looked up and smiled. "Is that okay?'

I patted her legs, heavy and limp in my lap and swallowed the tears that suddenly were choking my throat. "Fine," I said.

JoAnn called to David, who drove with the kids scrunched beside him in the front seat, "Turn here!! Go slow over the bumps! No sharp turns! Stay to the left!" By the time we arrived, we were all exhausted.

After we got her into the chair with pillows wedged around her, David and I took turns wheeling JoAnn around the sea wall path. Ari and Rachel put on their roller blades and skated ahead of us, up and back, whizzing around. I took in a breath of the salty air, as David pushed JoAnn ahead. Everyone suddenly looked small, like miniature figures moving against the backdrop of ocean and sky. When we came to a grassy slope that David couldn't push the wheelchair on, JoAnn climbed out, plodded up the hill, then settled back in with a sigh. Ari whispered to me, "If Aunt JoAnn can walk, then why is she in a wheelchair?"

I shrugged. " It hurts for her to walk. "

A week before she died, my mother had said to me, "If I had one wish it would be that JoAnn would get some help." In my family "help" meant counseling. My parents had sent JoAnn to a therapist when she was twelve. JoAnn says it was because they found she was sneaking out of the house at night to have sex with boys, but I'm never sure if what she says is true. I know the counseling didn't help—JoAnn was always wild and brazen, never appropriate.

When she married Greg at eighteen, it looked like she'd settled down. After college they moved to Canada to avoid the draft and go to graduate school. When the graduate fellowship she'd counted on didn't come through, her back pain started. Ice had to be fetched, then heating pads and pillows, then special foods and pills at all hours. Each year it got worse. More pillows, more treatments, more attention, with the world revolving around her in a slow dance that she directed. *Put the pillow under my left leg. Not at that angle.*

The morning we left Vancouver, David took out his guitar. JoAnn, who used to love to play guitar and sing, called out folksongs while David picked out chords. We all sang along, JoAnn loudest of all, her head lolling on her pillows, her eyes glowing. David finished with a song in Hebrew, a prayer for *Rafua shelema*, a complete healing. I joined him and we sang, "*Ana, Ayl na, Rafa na la, Ana, Ayl na, Rafa na la.* Heal our bodies, Open our hearts, Awaken our minds, *Shekhina*." We sang the lines over and over until JoAnn was singing with us, the kids were humming, and we chanted together, "Heal our Bodies, Open our hearts, Awaken our minds. *Shekhina*."

twenty-three

Even though Bubbe sleeps more and eats less now, she still rallies for visitors and can be remarkably alert. This afternoon when I hear a car in the driveway I look out the window to see Charu, an artist friend who visits Bubbe every Tuesday. At eighty years old, she is slim, white-haired, and dressed in jeans with a lime green flowered shawl slung around her shoulders.

A half hour later I go downstairs where Charu sits quietly next to Bubbe who is focusing intently on a paper at the table. Even though she probably can't see what she's drawing, Bubbe clutches a crayon and lets her arm trace flowing swirls of color until a picture emerges that looks like a flaming house dissolving into blue-green clouds.

Yesterday, when Rachel left the room, Bubbe called out, "Vere are you going?"

"To work on a school project."

"You're going to school? It's Sunday!" Bubbe hollered in disbelief. We all laughed. Who would think she'd know what day it is?

Doctor Robin Rose comes to visit on her day off and Bubbe grins as she squeezes her hand. "It's so vonderful dat you're a doctor, honey." When Robin sits on the bed and feels under Bubbe's red nightshirt with her stethoscope, Bubbe giggles. "I got de doctor in bed vit me!" After the exam, Bubbe announces, "You're de doctor, you've got to keep us all vell."

Robin says, "You've got to keep yourself well. Keep smiling."

I tell her Bubbe didn't smile much for the first hundred and two years of her life. This is hard for anyone to believe, because she's so sweet now. I think she has simply outlived her personality.

On Monday morning when she wakes, Bubbe clutches me and smiles into my face as I stroke her hair. Her smile grows more luminous as the rest of her drops away, as if something is blooming along with her dying, the layers peeling back to reveal a little more of something shiny and pure. Her love feels like a presence in the room. I couldn't feel that love when I was growing up, as if a thick veil separated us. Now everything is stripped away, cleaned bare so that when we're together, there's nothing else.

Bubbe beams at me again. Marilyn walks up behind us, clears her throat and says, "Yeah, she always has a smile for Debbie." I turn to see her stride over to the chair and bury her face in a magazine. I'm like the weekend father whose kids adore him, while Marilyn is the mom who does all the hard work and gets no credit. I understand how she feels, but I'm not sure how to handle her resentment. She has a huge heart, though, and even when she's worn out, she's as kind to Bubbe now as she was on her first day here.

Bubbe grows thinner and more ethereal each day, spiraling into a wraith as she wets her bed and sweats under her pile of blankets. With every meal she coughs, then smears food and sputum all over. When she pulls me toward her, sometimes I fight the urge to gag. She moans and I moan softly back, mirroring her voice. Her groans are like tiny calls for help, mine answers of reassurance. The further I go into her world, the harder it is to shift into the world of dealing with medication lists, hospice meetings, or caregivers' needs. After breathing softly next to Bubbe's cheek, I cringe when Marilyn pulls me aside and says, "I can't cook macaroni in this pot anymore! The lining is worn away, and everything sticks!" I take the pot in my hand, finger the crusty bottom, and nod dumbly while Bubbe gasps a gurgly breath, then grunts softly.

I go out to the mailbox to get a breath of spring air and find a letter from aunt Minnie. Instead of the monthly check she's enclosed a copy of a nasty letter she sent to Aunt Derril. *You are not contributing your fair share to Mother's living expenses!* It is filled with numbers with angry red circles scribbled around them. I feel my stomach churning. I want to wail, "Keep your fights to yourself! I have enough to manage with Bubbe!" Instead I sigh, and crumple the paper into a ball.

Later I moan to David, "I can't handle all this stuff. The more time I spend with Bubbe, the less patience I have with everything else."

He says, "Things come in packages—you get to be with Bubbe, but it comes with caregivers." I get to be with Bubbe, but it comes with Derril and Minnie's feud. I get to be with Bubbe, but it comes with prune juice dribble, diarrhea, three more trips to the grocery store every week and six lists of details to keep track of. She comes with a large package, yet her essence seems simpler everyday.

Rachel runs upstairs to tell me the orthopedic office is on the phone. My right shoulder has been bothering me for a couple of years, which we've finally discovered is due to a bone spur that showed up on my MRI last month. I've been waiting for a date for an arthroscopic surgery to shave it off.

"Doctor Townsend has a cancellation next week, and we can fit you in."

"You should do it," David says. He knows how much the shoulder has been hurting, waking me up at night for months.

"How can I handle a surgery with Bubbe here?" I stare at him.

"If you wait for her to die, it could be months."

I open my mouth to answer him, but suddenly I'm crying.

He puts his arm around my shoulder. "You have to take care of yourself."

I know he's right. The pain in my shoulder gets worse every day and the sooner I take care of it, the sooner it can heal, but it seems like crazy timing.

"We'll be at the hospital next Wednesday," I tell the nurse.

Later that evening as I pull into our driveway I see from the sliding-glass door that Bubbe is still sitting up in bed, so I go in.

She gazes at me "The vind is coming," she says. "The vind is coming. The vind is blowing us avay."

I nod and sing a few lines from the song, "Blowin' in the Wind."

She listens, and repeats, "The vind is blowing us avay."

"Oh, Bubbe, I hope you will go on a gentle, warm breeze."

She stares at me. "It's coming tonight. He's coming."

Upstairs later, getting ready for bed, I hear she's still talking loudly at midnight. I go down again to say goodnight. "Vat's new, honey?" she asks, as chipper as if it were nine a.m.

"I'm going to bed," I tell her firmly. "The kids are in bed, and you're going to bed, too."

"I'm already in bed," she laughs.

I begin to sing to her in Yiddish, "*Shluff mein kin, loo, loo, loo*" the way my mother would sing, late at night sometimes when I couldn't sleep. Even then I wanted to breathe in her faint lemony smell, inhale it deep enough so that I wouldn't forget her. She'd croon to the tune of Brahms' Lullaby, mixing a little English with the Yiddish. "*Shluff mein kin, loo, loo, loo. Shluff the ganze nacht through. . . Loo Loo Loo.*" During the day I was strong, the kind of daughter my mother needed, but once in a while, at night, I could be a girl who wanted lulling with a song. That song seeped through a chink in our world, a little Yiddish, a little English, drifting through generations. I hear the echo of my mother's voice now as I croon to Bubbe. "*Schluff mein kin. . . Loo Loo Loo.*" Bubbe sings it back to me, *Shluff mine kin, Sleep my child,* line by line, in the dark. We're like two drunks under a lamppost at midnight.

⌒

It's 1982. Rachel is nine months old and a friend of mine is arranging sessions with a woman who is supposed to be psychic. I don't believe in psychics, so I'm surprised when I hear myself say, "I want a session."

A few days later we sit down. Judy is tall and angular with a pale face and thick, dark hair. When she peers at me through black-framed librarian glasses, I feel edgy, like I'm going to the doctor.

"What's on your mind?" she asks. Her voice is a surprisingly strong baritone.

"My mother died seven years ago. Now that I have a baby, I keep wishing that my mother could see my daughter."

I pause, waiting for a response, but she just nods.

"I guess I was hoping you could tell me that my mother sees us. I want to know that she can see Rachel."

She brushes a hank of hair back from her face, and her eyes seem to grow larger behind the dark frames. "Why is it so important for you to know that your mother sees your child?"

I've been sitting prim on the edge of my chair, but now a knot in my chest begins to loosen and I start to weep. "I feel guilty for leaving my mother before she died. Maybe I want my daughter to be a peace offering." Between sobs, I tell her how I took care of my mother for a month before she died, then went back to Oregon, thinking I'd return after finals, but she died two weeks later.

"How old were you?" Judy asks.

"Twenty-three."

She stares at me. "You need to forgive yourself."

I don't get it. "I thought you were a psychic."

"Maybe. Mostly I'm intuitive."

I shake my head. "I don't know how to forgive myself."

"Go home. Find a place to be alone. Think back to what you went through. Remember how it felt to be losing her, how young and confused you were and already mourning while you took care of her. You had to leave to take care of *yourself*. There's nothing to feel guilty about."

I can't speak because I'm still crying.

"After that, picture yourself surrounded by light and picture your mother bathed in white light. Then speak to her."

Later in the afternoon while Rachel naps, I get in the bathtub. As soon as I'm in the warm water the sobbing starts again. I go back to that last month with my mother and my mind slides around the pain, how every day felt like a nightmare. How I ached with a sadness that I couldn't speak. Scenes float through my mind. The night we brought her home from the hospital, when my father gave her the first shot of pain medication, hands trembling, accidentally doubling the dose. Calling the ER, sitting up all night counting her breathing. Watching my father hold his grief, as if the shadow of her corpse had already entered his body, and he hauled it around, darkness in his face.

I watch my grandmother try to do something, anything, while her daughter is dying. I see my mother grope to find a way for her mother to give her something. "I want veal bird," my mother says, a dish I'd never heard of, but my grandmother brings it, and my mother eats it, nodding with each bite, yes, yes. Veal bird.

I watch my sister Nancy bring her four-year-old son to visit. I see Jeff howling at the bottom of the stairs, his blond curls damp with tears, refusing to come inside, afraid to see his grandma dying. Nancy torn. Everyone torn all around me. Then I see myself moving slowly, in a bad dream, unable to save my mother, unable to do anything.

I squeeze a washcloth over my head and let the water trickle down my chest until I feel something dissolving inside me, warm raindrops washing into a puddle. *Picture you and your mother surrounded by white light.* I want to do this. I want this burden to keep rinsing off. I close my eyes until I can see myself, fuzzy white around me, and try to picture my mother. Her face appears, healthy and fleshed out again, framed by short dark hair. I don't know if it's real or in my mind and I don't care. I want to be forgiven, I want to be in white light where things are fair and come out even. The weight in my chest needs to keep dissolving. My mother smiles at me through tears.

"I'm sorry," I say. The words make a flat ping against the bathtub tiles. "I just couldn't stay with you until the end. I had to go home for a while."

"It's all right." My mother's voice floats like cotton around her face, everything white, fuzzy. "There's nothing to be sorry for."

"I have a baby now," I tell her. "Rachel Bernice. Can you see her? Can you see how beautiful she is?"

My mother's eyes shift into focus, as if she sees me. "I can see her," she says. She *is* beautiful. And you're a good mother."

⌒

Bubbe's voice has faded to a whisper and her chest sounds like a murky pond, gurgling with every breath. Last night Karen let her sit up until she was so overtired that she wouldn't let anyone near her. "Get away! Get away!" she hollered. When Rachel came downstairs, she got her to muster a little smile and convinced her to let Karen help her into bed. Later when I came to say goodnight, she yelled, "Get away!" It frightened me, making me think that in the end she'll push us all away. I've had visions of her dying peacefully in my arms, but now I fear it won't be so easy. A few days ago when she slept all day I thought she'd lapse into a coma, but the next day she was wide-awake, and "herself" again. After shrieking at everyone last night, she awoke this morning docile, pleased to have company.

Today she reaches for me and pulls me to her heart, like a soft, wounded creature. I feel the heat of her fear as she breathes. Her muffled cries seem to come from beneath an ocean, each breath rapid and intense as childbirth. But this is death, not birth, that beckons. *Don't worry, Bubbe*, I want to tell her, *it will be all right*. But the truth is it scares me too, as she sits so close to the unknown.

When I walk down the stairs a few hours later I see her still sitting at the table, wrapped in the thin gray airplane blanket saved from her trip here. On that plane I gripped her hand as we wrapped her in more blankets, as if we could protect her frail body from the shock of the journey, all the changes to come. Her hands tremble now as she grabs for her dreidle. It spins, wobbling, falling, wobbling, slowly dropping, again and again.

Later I wake from a nap on my office couch. Images of my mother and my great-grandmother fade with the wisps of a dream. I close my eyes again and let Rose and Bernice drift back into my mind. *They lead me to a cave, slowly, one on each side, holding my hands. Inside it is bloody and warm, filled with the rushing of water and heartbeats. Lena is cradled in my arms, but mingled with me so I'm not sure who is who. I hold her body carefully in front of me, feeling its weight. My tears slide into the warm tears of Rose and Bernice, forming a stream that will carry Bubbe on her journey.*

When I go upstairs, I take out my "Earth Voices" deck, spread the cards out, and draw:

The Cave of Initiation: "There is no turning back. Here you commit to die and be reborn. . .If you are not ready, pick another card."

PART IV

The Cave of Initiation

There is no turning back. Here you commit to die and be reborn
To deepen and illumine
You are supported by all the elements
Perfectly balanced at the Source.
If you are not ready to pass beyond this entrance,
put this card back and draw another.

–Earth Voices, Robert Beridha

twenty-four

March, 1997

A deep ache spreads from my armpit to my shoulder blade as I hunch over, guarding my arm. I had the shoulder surgery two days ago, and today I breathe slowly as if to exhale traces of anesthesia and the faint dream of being sliced into that leaves me trembly.

Marilyn comes up the stairs and knocks on the door.

"I need a break," she says.

I've stayed upstairs, avoiding Bubbe since I came home from the hospital because of the way she can peer into me, like a laser, to the pain. The pills I'm taking numb the sting around my shoulder, but they don't erase the feeling of being exposed to the bone. David and Rachel have covered Marilyn's breaks for the last couple of days, but they've gone back to school and work. "I don't want her to see me like this," I tell Marilyn, pointing to my sling. "Can you wait 'til she's asleep?" Marilyn nods.

When Bubbe dozes dozes off, Marilyn goes out to take Buddy for a walk. I open the door to Bubbe's room and keep watch from the top of the stairs, tiptoeing back and forth, peering down the stairwell at her bed while I cradle my arm. It feels as if she sees me in her sleep like a great Cyclops crone with one eye bulging from the middle of her forehead. I sneak around, avoiding that powerful gaze.

That night I sleep fitfully, the pain in my shoulder waking me up every time I shift my body. In the morning, I hear Diane, the hospice nurse visiting, so I take off my sling and go downstairs. Bubbe is wide awake, sitting at the table cramming her mouth with pancakes and syrup, and chattering to Diane at the same time. "Hev a little to eat, honey." She urges. Diane laughs. I already had breakfast," she says, as Bubbe waves the fork in front of her.

When I walk over Bubbe looks up and beams at me, "How's da femmily?" She reaches out and pats my shoulder.

"We're fine," I say, pulling my shoulder away, pretending to tidy the table.

"Vell, let's hev a party!" Bubbe giggles as the three of us gape at her.

She pushes herself back from the table, grabs her walker, hoists herself up without any help, and starts tottering around the room.

"Bubbe, Where are you going?" Marilyn rushes after her.

Bubbe stops at the sliding glass door, pivots with her walker and announces, "If I vas a little younger, I'd go out and get a job!"

Diane says that people often have bursts of energy before they die. Bubbe keeps this up most of the day, chattering and laughing and getting up and down. In the late afternoon she is winding down, sitting in her bed, looking around and fidgeting. I sit with her for a while, but she can't really carry on a conversation. She seems lost, her eyes darting around the room as she repeats, "Vere shall I take it? Vat do I give?"

"Bubbe," I grasp her hand firmly until her eyes settle on me. "Do you want to play cards?" Maybe this will give her a focus.

"Oh sure I do!" She's delighted by the idea.

I pull an old deck of cards from the desk drawer. "You're the one who taught me how to play," I tell her.

She stares back at me. "Who me? Naw!"

"Yes, you taught me Gin Rummy and Casino." She furrows her brow, struggling to recall. "And you always let me win." She laughs.

As I deal a hand of Casino, I see the maple dining room table in her house in North Hollywood, sense the faces gazing at us from the pale photos on the walls. Bubbe would throw away good cards, making obvious mistakes. "Grandma," I'd plead, "you don't have to let me win. I'm not a baby." She'd shrug and glance away.

Bubbe clutches her hand now and looks baffled. "Vat do I give?" she says, as she stares at the cards on the bedside table. "Vat do I give?" I reach over and gently play her hand for her until I see she's getting too frustrated. I fold up the cards and announce, "You won, Bubbe."

"Really?"

"No, I let you win. Now it's my turn to let you win."

The next night when we light candles, Bubbe's too confused to remember the Shabbat blessings. She eats only a few bites of dinner, and falls into a deep sleep for twenty-four hours. When she wakes she wags her head and blinks spasmodically as if she's trying to clear a blurry TV screen in her head. She repeats, "Someting's wrong. Someting's wrong in da femmily."

"Everything's okay, Bubbe," I tell her. "You just slept a whole night and day."

She stares at me. "Did I die?"

"No, I don't think so."

"Am I dying?"

I hesitate. "Maybe. What do you think?"

"I don't know." She stares at her hands.

"Are you ready to die, Bubbe?"

"I don't know."

I speak slowly about where she lives and who we are, to anchor her back. We look at photos of us smiling with the Chanukah lights, then flip through her old photo album, naming who is still in this world and who has crossed over. Bubbe's fingers pause on a photo of my mother holding me when I was a baby. "Dat's Debbie vit Rachel," she says. She glances at me and back to the photo.

"No, it's my mother with me. It's Bernice."

Bubbe shakes her head. "Bernice is gone, honey."

I nod. "She's been dead twenty-two years now." As I say it, I realize it's my mother's *yartzeit* this week, the anniversary of her death.

"Det's a nice picture." Bubbe peers closer. She strokes it like an old trinket and sighs.

A nice picture of a smiling mother holding a pretty child in front of a house, but I can see the baby isn't smiling. Suddenly, my stomach feels queasy, like I've swallowed something rotten. I don't want to go in that house again.

In the bedroom inside the house the shades are drawn, but the afternoon light curls around the corners of the blinds and colors the room a pale yellow. The baby sleeps in her crib. The pink blanket wrapped around her is frayed at the edges where she sucks on it in her sleep.

She stirs, when she hears voices rising, feels someone moving in the room. She stuffs the blanket in her mouth and sucks harder.

She hears voices rise. Hears Nancy screaming. She sees JoAnn coming at Nancy, a shadow on the bedroom wall. The yelling vibrates and echoes off the walls as the baby tugs at her ear and chews the blanket into a wrinkled, wet shape.

The crib rails rattle, as her mother comes in and slams the door shut. The yelling is louder, the room hot. Her mother grabs JoAnn's and Nancy's heads and bangs them together. The shapes on the wall flicker and the screams come from far away. The baby rolls over and sucks the blanket into a wad. A damp stain spreads over the corners of her mouth.

I want to reach through the photo and lift myself out of my mother's arms. *Maybe you did the best you could,* I'd tell her, *but you didn't take care of me. You used to say, "Have a third baby. They're the best!" But you didn't know how hard I worked to be that good baby for you.* I swallow down the sour taste in my mouth as the picture comes into focus. It's easy to see why I never feel I have support and how quick I am to think that David has abandoned me. He's a safe target for my feelings, but he's never actually left me. It was my mother, smiling as she holds me in the photo, who abandoned me from the start.

Bubbe runs her fingers over the photo again. "Det vas so long ago, honey," she says.

I nod, "It was."

No one thought Bubbe would make it this far, but Purim has arrived, the holiday that celebrates Queen Esther rescuing the Jews. Every year we dress in costumes and put on a Purim shpiel, a comic version of the book of

Esther. We boo at the villain, Haman, and cheer for the hero, Mordechai, and heroine, Esther. I agreed to tell the Purim story this year, but it feels odd to be coming out of Bubbe's death chamber and dressing up as a middle-eastern queen. I tell David, "I don't know if I can do this."

"If you really can't, then don't," he says. "But maybe it'll be good for you to get on stage and have a good time."

A good time. Why not? The anti-inflammatory medicine for my shoulder has kicked in just enough so that I can gesture, and I've got two friends from my theatre group helping me.

I stand on stage at the Community Center hall that we've rented for the event and look out at the crowd. A few clowns, a conehead, several queens, and an assortment of belly dancers. As the story begins, I exaggerate the foolish king, the wicked villain, and the young, clueless Esther entering the palace. Dana and Judy behind me pantomime the drunken king hiccupping, Esther prancing around in a beauty contest, and Haman groveling and sneering. The audience cheers and hisses. When they boo at Haman, everybody shakes *gragers*, noisemakers that make a grinding racket. This is one occasion when I don't have a silent audience.

Suddenly I feel Esther stumbling onto her destiny as she enters the palace, and I can't help but think of Bubbe coming to our home, not knowing what was ahead. She called to me, and here I am, worn out from caring for her, wishing it was over, standing on stage and staring at a bunch of clowns. I catch a glimpse of David wearing a goofy black wig and beard with his Brooklyn Dodgers uniform. He gives me a thumbs-up.

As Esther prepares to reveal herself to the King, I chant, *Esther fasted, she held her vision before her, she did not feed her body, she fed the strength of her soul.* When the moment comes for her to come forward to save her people, the audience chants with me, *Now is the Time Esther, Now is the Time. It is your Destiny.* I step forward as Esther goes before the king. *She rose before the King . . . in all her beauty, in all her strength, in all her power.* I raise my arms slowly as I walk to the front of the stage. A quivery current moves up my spine as I plant my feet. It might be an adrenaline surge from the crowd cheering, but suddenly I can lift my arm higher than I could all week. The audiences cheers.

Later, at home, we head downstairs to show Bubbe our costumes. Rachel and her friend Sarah, dressed as Raggedy Ann and Andy in bright red wigs with polka-dot cheeks, pirouette in front of Bubbe's bed. She sits straight up. "A Purim party!" Her eyes widen as she hollers, "I vant to go to da party!"

Diane says that the increase in the pain medication might explain the seesawing between bursts of energy and lapses of confusion as her body adjusts to the change. In between the high periods, she's disoriented and jabbers in Yiddish, staring at nothing. She's been so weak the last few days that she can hardly bear any weight on her feet. Now suddenly she grins wildly, hoists herself up to the side of the bed, and yells again: "I vant to go to the party, gals!" We laugh. I'm tired and confused too, yet tonight, like Bubbe, I had a burst of energy. We're groping through this together, sprinting towards the finish line, collapsing, then picking ourselves up and moving on.

twenty-five

On Sunday morning I jump out of bed when I hear a pounding on our bedroom door. Karen stands in the doorway, her tall frame tense, her hazel eyes lined with dark circles like a frightened ghost.

"Bubbe was up all night, trying to climb out of bed!"

"Is she okay?" I grab my robe.

Karen's hands are shaking. "I found her on the floor twice, and got her back in bed. Once she had her head stuck between the bedrails and the mattress!"

"And now?'

"She's in bed, but she has bruises."

I rush downstairs where Bubbe is collapsed on the bed, breathing slowly, like a weary warrior after a fight. Against the pale flannel sheets, I see the delicate skin on her arm is stained dark amber and blue. Karen is still trembling. "I know Marilyn will blame me," she says.

I hug Karen and feel how thin and frail her shoulders are. "It's not your fault." I tell her. I promise to come down when Marilyn arrives so we can explain what happened together.

We lean over Bubbe's bed on either side and press the blankets snugly into the mattress so she can't get out. Bubbe groans in her sleep as we stuff the railings with extra quilts for padding. I call Diane who tells us to reduce the pain medication, since it could be causing the agitation. Bubbe doesn't seem to be able to tolerate too much of any drug, be it morphine, codeine, or any derivative. With smaller doses, though, she's still in a lot of pain.

I try not to panic, but I keep seeing Bubbe's bruises, so dark against her papery skin. Something inside me feels jostled, as if a picture in my head has been jarred out of focus, spinning out of control. We brought Bubbe here to die cocooned in love and comfort, maybe even to soothe old hurts, but now her body smarts with fresh wounds.

When she wakes a few hours later, I come down to see her propped up against her pillows, staring into space and mumbling. I lean in close, reach over the rails, and gently stroke her bruised arm. "How are you Bubbe?"

She stares past me and rattles on in Yiddish. *Gevult. . . mit mein. . .fergin* . . .The words fly from her mouth in a jumbled stream; her face is tilted, her eyes glazed. She's like an extra-terrestrial, bobbing her swollen head on her bony shoulders, sliding into another dimension. I stay with her, stroke her hand, wanting to lead her back, but she babbles on.

As the medication level recedes in the next days, she grows still, the alien creature retreating as she inhabits herself again. She sleeps more, though, and can hardly bear weight or move on her own.

For the first time I'm hoping for Bubbe to die.

I'm ashamed to admit it, but I'm ready to reclaim my life and she's still here. Since my shoulder surgery I feel as if parts of me have come unfastened, and I need a quiet, calm place to gather myself. The kids are out of school for spring break and the house is jammed with bodies, voices, demands. No solitude in sight.

In the first months of Bubbe's crash-landing in our home and the flurry of activity that came with it, I stayed afloat partly because of the sense of being "called" to do this. Once she settled in, I was fed by the feel of her gnarled hand, her soft cheek, the quiet moments we shared. Then came dreamy visions about the womb-cave and journeying backward through menstrual blood with ancestors for guides. The reality now is that Bubbe jabbers in Yiddish, tears off her bedclothes and falls out of bed. We can't stop her suffering, and she's still alive.

David walks into the bedroom where I sit on the edge of the bed, still in my nightgown, staring into space. He sits down next to me. "What's going on?"

"I'm running out of steam."

"Meaning?"

I don't feel like I can help Bubbe anymore, keep the caregivers happy, or keep myself in one piece."

"Well, we have to think of some solutions." David adjusts his glasses.

"Like what? Either she dies soon or I check into a sanitarium. That's all I can think of."

David strokes my shoulder and speaks softly. "Well, we could put her in a nursing home."

"This whole idea was to get her *out* of the nursing home."

"That was five months ago. We could find her a nicer facility here, hire special one-on-one care and go visit her a few times a week." He points out that she'd still be far better off than she was in Los Angeles and I could get my bearings back.

I shake my head. It's so like him to be able to detach and think of a logical solution without feeling the least bit guilty. To even think of doing that makes me feel like I've not only failed a test, but gotten up and walked out of the class.

I've been wanting to plant spring flowers, craving anything new and blooming, but there's been no time. Bubbe is awake and calm again this afternoon so I decide to bring her out with me while I garden, and Rene helps me bundle her into the wheelchair. She stares up at me as I lean in and tuck blankets around her lap. "Let's go outside, Bubbe," I say, smiling into her face.

"Vat's outside?" she glances suspiciously at the window. We gaze at the tiny flecks of dust floating through the stream of sunlight into the room.

"It's spring. We can get some fresh air."

"Fresh air?" She shrugs. "I need more den fresh air, honey."

I wheel her out to the porch landing where she can see me planting a few steps below. She shifts her weight and blinks in the light as I sift the earth from one pot to another, settling in the seedlings.

"Look, Bubbe!" I shout to her. I hold up a bright purple pansy and wave it above my head. She gazes at the flash of color in the air and nods. I dig into the dirt, settle the root ball in the hole, and gently tamp the fresh soil around it. When I look up again, her eyes are half closed, and she's snoring.

twenty-six

On Wednesday morning Rene runs down the hall, bangs on our door and yells, "Debbie, come quick!" I race downstairs to find Bubbe lying on the carpet next to the bed with her head propped on a crumpled pillow, breathing softly, but motionless.

Rene says, "I tried to lift her to the commode, but her legs buckled and I couldn't hold her weight, so I slid her down as slowly as I could and ran to get you."

"You did the right thing," I say. I stare at Bubbe resting on the floor, her pale legs flopping out from her flowery pink nightgown. Her wizened face is perched on the pillow, her eyes staring into space. Maybe it's the wave of panic rising in me that makes the room look huge with Bubbe lost in the middle, tiny and helpless.

I breathe slowly, clasp my hands together to stop trembling, and smile reassuringly at Rene. Together, we bend and scoop Bubbe's slack body into our arms. My shoulder is still weak, so I lean in with my left side and bend my knees. We count to three, and carefully lift her back into bed as she groans. Once in bed, she opens her eyes wide and glares up at us, as if we've disturbed her dream. She's too low in the bed, so we grasp her undersheet from each side, a technique I learned years ago in the nursing home, and slide her to the top. Her eyes bulge as I lean over her, and she reaches up and smacks me in the face with her fist. Hard.

I reel backward. Tears spring to my eyes, but I turn and blink them away, trying to stay calm. Rene runs and gets a cold washcloth, which I press to my cheek.

"Are you all right?" she asks.

I take a deep breath and nod.

For a moment we just stare while Bubbe turns her head away, as if the score is settled, and starts to snore. This feels like a bad dream where the air is so thick I have to move slowly to see what's coming. I breathe deeply again as I turn from the bed and show Rene how to lift Bubbe next time. *Bend your knees* I say, as I demonstrate a slow deliberate plie, but my knees are trembling. *Hold your abdominal muscles tight* I tell her, but I can barely feel my own breathing. *Call me to help anytime.*

The tears fall as I climb the stairs. When I get into the living room, I'm sobbing. I stop to catch my breath, and realize the house is eerily quiet with everyone still dozing at seven in the morning.

I know Bubbe didn't mean to hurt me. She just struck out in her helplessness at whoever was moving her against her will. Maybe she can't remember much or walk anymore, but she still delivers a good punch. The sting of her fist on my cheek stays with me all day, like a sharp echo.

I've hardly ever been hit. I have hazy memories of my mother and sisters hitting each other when I was a baby, but they didn't hit me. As I feel the imprint of Bubbe's hand on my cheek, I cannot imagine the toll of her mother hitting her so regularly took on her.

⌒⌐

Russia, 1900

Lena is seven years old. She lives near the Polish border, sometimes called Russia, sometimes Poland. The cotton dress that droops to her ankles is anchored by an apron slashed around her middle. The big clothes make her face seem smaller, darker, under the tangle of curls that peek out from her kerchief.

She dips a spoon into a pot of cornmeal on the stove, and offers it to the baby balanced on her hip. Her little brother Jack, just seven months old, wriggling in her arms, seems almost as big as Lena, and threatens to tip her over as he grabs the spoon and waves it over his head. Lena laughs and wipes the cornmeal off his cheeks. She sits down and places him on the floor to play while she catches her breath. She still has to clean the kitchen and sweep the floor when he takes a nap. It could be a long time until he settles down, so she looks around for something more to occupy him.

She glances out the window, and sees the tall green blades of a windmill, turning, *click, whoosh, turn, click, whoosh, turn*. Her mother, Rose, bought the windmill this week, another of her plans to start a business, wheel and deal, grind flour, make ends meet, and put food on the table.

In a small square of a window near the top of the windmill she can see just a shadow of Rose hunched over a table. The blades turn, *click, whoosh, turn*. Jack scoots over, tugs at Lena's s skirt, tries to pull himself to standing, but topples over and howls. Lena scoops him up, and says, "Let's go see Mama in the windmill!" Jack stops howling and studies her face. "Ma-Ma," he says.

She wraps a blanket around him before they step into the damp wind. They moved into this house by the edge of a river just last week because the rent is lower than in the village and Rose got a deal on it if she'd run the windmill. A few other weathered shacks are scattered along the bank. To Lena they look weary and lonely, like they might all heave a sigh and just slide into the river. She misses the village, where the streets were full of people, and around the corner another family that spoke Yiddish let her come in and play with their children. The mother would smile at her and say, "Come in, little *mameleh*, how is the *tatteleh* today?" She would even lift Jack out of Lena's arms so she could run to play with the other children. Here, by the dark river, where the wet wind turns the blades of the windmill, it is lonely.

Jack points his fist at the spinning blades. "Ma-Ma!" he calls again. Lena hugs him close as she runs to the door of the windmill. She pushes it open and calls up the stairs, "Mama! Can we come up?" Rose doesn't answer. Lena is careful to wipe her feet on the rags at the foot of the stairs. She knows her mother will holler if she gets mud inside. "*Vilde Chaya!* Wild beast!" she'll say. "Who do you think will clean up your mess?"

On the stairway Lena feels the thudding of the blades as they turn. It's like walking inside an enormous clock, ticking and whirring. She matches her footsteps to the pulse of the clock in her mind. *Skip, jump, step, tick*. At the top she sees a patch of light where her mother sits by the window. A huge wheel at the center spins slowly. As Lena skips up the last stair, Rose turns, and shakes her head. "I told you to stay in the house. Are you deaf?" Her face softens when Jack reaches to her. She takes him onto her lap. "*Paschke, Paschke.*" She pats his hands together as he laughs. "Here." She thrusts him back to Lena. "I have work to do. Do you think I have time to play with a baby all day?"

Lena walks to the window and looks out. "Mama, you can see all the way across the river from here!" Jack tugs on Lena's hair. She sets him down next to her mother and places her hand on the windowsill. If she squints hard enough, maybe she can see the village on the other side of the river. Maybe that's the smoke rising from smokestacks, on the street they lived on, maybe it's just on the other side. If she narrows her eyes into slits, she can make out a house, even people on the street.

She hears her mother scream as if from far away across the river, and she turns before she hears the baby tumbling down the stairs, *tick, click, whirr, bang,* Jack howls, Rose bellows, *tick, click, whirr, bang.* If she squeezes her eyes shut and puts her hand over her ears, she will not hear the crash at the bottom of the steps. Just the whoosh of the blades and the roar of the river.

Rose races to the bottom of the stairs, where the baby is screaming. His nose is bloody and he has a soft red bump on his chin that is turning a deep purple, like a plum going rotten. Rose clutches him and roars, "My Jacov! My beautiful little *yingele!*" Then she turns to Lena who is scrambling away. She yanks her by the hair and jerks her to the bottom stair. "You stupid girl! You were supposed to watch him!" With Jack cradled in one arm, she twists Lena's wrist and pulls her outside and back to the house. She wraps Jack tight in a blanket, rocks and sings to him, "*Schluff mine kind, loo, loo, loo, schluff mine shayna yingele,*" until his eyes close.

Lena hunches in the corner, crying softly. When Rose turns to her she tries to make herself shrink, but it's no use. The first blow hits her on the side of the head, and as she slips to the floor, she tries to crawl under the bed, but Rose grabs her ankle and yanks her back. She slams her fist into Lena's back, just between the shoulder blades, and screams "He could be dead, my Jacov, for all you care, you stupid, senseless girl!"

Rose shoves Lena's head into the floor until she tastes the sour grit from the dirt and her spit leaves a muddy stain. If she is limp like a dead fish and doesn't make a sound, it will be over sooner. But Rose is angrier than usual, her voice rising over the roar of the river, "Don't ever turn your back on him again!" She grabs Lena's hair again, wrenches her head up off the floor and kicks her in the ribs. "Do you hear me?"

When Rose slams the door and goes back out, Lena crawls up into the bed with Jack, who whimpers in his sleep. She pulls him close like a doll, and breathes into his chest. She runs her fingers over the dark bruise on his chin, as she twirls her finger around one of his curls. She counts the rhythm of the windmill spinning, *click, turn, whoosh, click turn, whoosh.* She imagines she is riding on the windmill to the other side of the river . . . *click, turn, whoosh, click, turn* . . . until she sleeps.

A week after Bubbe's fall, her wrist is still dark blue and magenta, and there are amber bruises on her knee and above her eyebrow. I hunch close as we talk, my head almost resting on the bed with her. "You know," she says as she peers at me, "you look a lot like Debbie."

"That's good, Bubbe," I say, "because I *am* Debbie." We laugh.

She pauses, then stares at me again, tilting her head. "Look at dose bleck eyes. . . a lot like Debbie's eyes."

"Well, I do look like Debbie," I tell her. "You know, *you* remind me of Bubbe." She laughs again. I lean in and study the deep lines on her face, etched like an intricate map. I wish I could read the map more clearly, see into her mind.

Marilyn tells me that when Bubbe was frustrated last night, she said, "God take me, already." They chanted together, "Please God, take me. Please God, take me," over and over.

I'm praying to God to take her, too. It doesn't seem fair for someone so fierce and strong to have to struggle and waste away indefinitely. Actually it's me, I realize, who can't stand to watch her disintegrate in front of me. Seeing her fall, feeling her hit me, wondering when she'll let go.

twenty-seven

The next morning Bubbe wakes in a nasty mood, constipated. When I come in she's lying in bed half-naked with the covers off.

"What's going on?" I ask Karen, who sits in a chair near the bed.

Karen sighs and says, "She keeps pulling off her clothes and picking at her bottom."

When I walk up to the bed, Bubbe screams, "GET AVAY! I'M SICK!" and swings her fists in the air. This is a gesture I take seriously now, so I back up.

While Karen and I talk, a safe distance from the bed, Bubbe manages to pick some feces from her bottom and smear them on the bed rail. I run for some soapy washrags so Karen can scrub Bubbe's hands while I scour the rail. All the while, Bubbe yells and flails at us, "GET AVAY! GET AVAY!"

This goes on for about an hour until we decide to give her a suppository to get it over with. I lean in close and hold Bubbe's hands firmly while Karen inserts it. She stares up at me, then her eyes narrow, and she screeches, "YOU'RE MY MOTHER!" I stumble away from the bed, shaking. A few minutes later, when her eyes find me across the room, she hollers "GET AVAY, MY MOTHER!"

My grandmother told me so many stories of how her mother beat her that even though I never met my Great-grandmother Rose, she lurked in the back of my mind like a shadow. She appeared accidentally three years ago at a storytelling workshop when the teacher asked us to visualize portraits of our ancestors, as if we were visitors in a family gallery. I closed my eyes, breathed, felt my body sink into the floor, and let my mind float.

I see heavy oil portraits hanging on a white wall. My mother's cheeks are creamy peach-tinted, her hair piled in a dark wave. There's my Grandma Lena, standing straight in a navy blue, stiff-collared dress, her hand posed on a high-backed blue velvet chair. I scan the wall. There's my aunt Sadie. . . and my great-grandma, Rose. My eyes lock into hers so I can't turn away. She's a massive ammunition tank of a woman with broad flat cheeks and a stony stare. I search her face for an ounce of compassion, but there's no mercy here, not even for a great-granddaughter who has stumbled onto her in the dark.

I hear the teacher's voice. "Now focus on one of the portraits, and feel yourself going deeper into that person." *I'm cold. I want to leave, but there's nowhere to go. Rose grasps me with her gaze.*

"Feel yourself merging with the flesh of that person, until you know what it's like to be in her skin." *I don't want to go into her darkness, but my body is going, my mind following.* "Hold yourself in the posture of that person." *I feel my shoulders tighten and my jaw clamp as an icy hatred seeps through my body, traveling from my feet into my chest. I'm so shaken that I begin to cry, but I still feel it. Meanness, and hate.*

"Just let it be, sit with it," advises the teacher. *Then I feel a toughening in my gut, as my pores tingle and contract. I hear a flat voice inside me say, "Don't mess with me."*

"Now allow yourself to go back in time, to feel this person's experiences." *I see myself surrounded by young men, my brothers. They taunt me, poke at me, ridicule me. They come at me over and over until I feel a rage bubble up and something hot hardens in my veins. The voice says, "I won't let you hurt me." I sneer, my heart turns and shrinks as my fists clench. "I won't be weak like a girl." That thought swirls in my head, swivels, and lodges in my heart. I will not be female. I will be just as tough as they are—no, tougher. My skin will harden to a hide.*

I'm sitting in Rose's body at the moment of that decision, and I get it. In my bones I understand that when she gave birth to a girl, she berated her and beat her. Later that daughter, Lena, would smash her daughter Minnie's cradle, and my mother would knock my sisters' heads together, and on and on. I don't hate Rose now or fear her, because I *am* her. *I whisper softly to her. "I'm sorry. I'm so sorry."*

Bubbe hollers again, "Get avay, my mother!" as I walk toward her bed. The suppository hasn't worked, except for a small softening that allowed her to smear more feces over the sheets and bedrails. I look Bubbe in the eye and stand very still.

"I'm *Debbie,*" I say, as I show her two yellow laxative tablets in the palm of my hand.

She stares back, silent.

"These will make you feel better." I nod firmly as I place them in her hand.

Karen hands Bubbe a glass of prune juice and she miraculously puts the tablets in her mouth and swallows them. Her mood improves in a few hours when the pills start to take effect. She then moves her bowels about five times during the night. After going to a wedding in the evening, I come home at midnight to see the lights on in Bubbe's room. I go in to help Karen change the bedding, wipe Bubbe's bottom, lift her to the commode again, and scrape the feces from her fingernails one more time. After scrubbing the bedrails and dropping the third set of sheets in the washer, I climb up the stairs to bed.

Bubbe sleeps most of the next day, exhausted by this ordeal. I'm weary and shaky all day, too, and feel something slipping inside me. Lying on the couch in the middle of the day, my body feels heavy like lead, but my mind won't rest. When the phone rings, I answer it to hear an oddly familiar voice. It's a childhood friend of my mother's who I haven't seen in twenty years. Her speech is slurred from a car accident long ago that left her partly paralyzed. "Debb-eee," she says, elongating the sounds with a kind of thudding rhythm. "I just waant-ed to tell you what a wond-er-ful thing you are doo-ing for your grand-ma. We all ad-mire you so much, and you will be re-ward-ed for what you are doo-ing. It is such a *mitz-vah.*"

twenty-eight

All through the night I wake from fragmented dreams. I can't remember what I dreamed, but the wisps seem to float just out of reach, waiting to be gathered into meaning. I'm tense and grouchy all day.

This afternoon I'm trying to nap, when I hear Ari in the driveway. I look out the window to see him plop his bike on the concrete and race into the house. I holler, "Go back and put your bike on the side of the house where it belongs and lock it!"

His head is buried in the refrigerator by the time I get downstairs, and for a second it looks like the wrong kid in my house. His jeans are so baggy and low-slung that they could slide to the floor with one tug. He clutches the cuffs on his sweatshirt like big oven mitts as he reaches for the peanut butter. A desperate little refugee in outsized clothes. There's still a trace of sweetness in his face but it's hard to see under his long, streaked hair.

He barely pulls his head out as he mumbles, "Chill out, Mom. I'll do it later." He waves a hand behind him as if to shoo me away. He probably won't put the bike away, but I'm too tired to argue, so I sit down at the kitchen table.

"How was school today?" I ask him.

"Lame, as usual."

"Have you got homework?"

"Not much. I just have to read some of that stupid book and do some math."

"Which stupid book?"

"The one about the rabbits. It's supposed to be about how people act and governments and stuff. I think it's just about a bunch of rabbits running around and talking. It's so boring."

Literary metaphor escapes Ari. But really, his direct simplicity is what I love about him. A rabbit is a rabbit.

"I could help you with the reading if you want."

"Naah, thanks anyway." Ari slides off his chair and leaves his sandwich half-eaten on his plate on the table.

"Put your plate in the dishwasher!"

My words reach him just as he gets to the stairs. He wheels around.

"God, Mom! I have to make a phone call right now! I'll be back in a minute!"

We used to read together every night. *The Indian in the Cupboard, Harris and Me, Hatchet.* Boy books. Adventure, action, mystery. We'd lie on my bed, cozy, often reading until he'd fall asleep. David would carry him into his own bed later. In the mornings he'd crawl back into our bed before school, his hair tousled, his brown eyes bright. Cuddle up between us, talk about the day. What's for breakfast? Will you pick me up for soccer practice?

In middle school he's a new man, no reading, no snuggling. I pick up his sandwich and throw it in the trash, toss his dish into the sink, then trudge up the stairs. As I pass his room, I hear him talking on the phone. "Awesome," he says. "That is soo dope."

When he hears me walk by he yells, "Mom, would you shut my door?"

"NO! You can do *that* all by yourself!" I go in my room, collapse on the bed, and press my face into the pillow. Marilyn's voice below me is shrill, wheedling, loud enough for Bubbe to hear. *Eat your pancakes, honey. One more bite.* I can't tune her out.

Earlier in the week she asked for more time off because she's overworked and needs more breaks. I explained that we could give her more time off, but it has to be a twenty-four-hour shift, since it's too difficult and expensive to train someone to fill in short daytime hours.

She glared at me and said, "That won't work for me."

Now she seems mad at me all the time, keeping up a constant litany of complaints. *Those vegetables aren't organic. Karen fed Bubbe tuna fish and it gave her a stomachache. The hospice aide didn't clean Bubbe's toenails. Tell Ari not to play his music so loud.*

My eyes are closed, but I still hear her below me and Ari laughing on the phone in his bedroom. I put in my earplugs and count backward from one hundred until I drift off. The ringing phone wakes me. Maybe it's the hospice nurse calling me back because we need to adjust Bubbe's medication again.

"Is Ari there?" It's a giggly girl's voice.

I stumble into the hallway and call to Ari to pick up the phone. "You have five minutes," I tell him. "Then *I* need the phone and you need to do your homework."

"I don't have any homework!" he hollers back. "Would you get off my case?" His door slams shut.

I bang on the door. "You do have homework! You told me you do! You can't talk on the phone all day!

"Leave me alone! GET OUT OF MY LIFE, MOM!"

I hear myself beginning to scream, "OPEN UP THIS DOOR! YOU CANNOT SLAM IT IN MY FACE! I *am* in your life! I am still your mom! If you think you are going to get through school on your good looks and not do your work you have another thing coming!" I'm still knocking on the door and I can't stop. I just keep hollering and banging. I hear Ari yelling back, but I don't care. I hear myself yelling louder, "WHO DO YOU THINK YOU ARE? You never listen to anyone! I can't do this anymore! I can't fight with you anymore! I AM SO SICK OF YOUR RUDENESS!" I keep pounding until my fist is numb. Then I sit on the floor. Suddenly it is very quiet except for the sound of Ari sniffling inside his room, and another sound I realize is my own crying. Rachel stands behind me, staring. David comes up the stairs. He helps me up off the floor and leads me into the bedroom.

Later I call my friend Rebecca to tell her I can't go to her anniversary party that evening. "My nerves are shot," I tell her. David insists that Ari come with him to the party so I can have some time alone. Later he admits he didn't want to leave Ari home with me.

Minneapolis, 1913

On a damp February afternoon Lena, bundled in a shawl, hugs her new baby close, little Sol. Her daughter Minnie, born on Lena's eighteenth birthday, is a year and a half now, a toddler in constant motion. Lena pulls the blanket from Sol's face as she steps into the house. His cheeks are pink and squinched like a little old *Zayde*, a grandpa. He makes her think of her younger brother Jack, so many years ago.

Her neighbor brought her home from the hospital where for two days she was relieved to lie on the bed and nurse the baby while they brought her meals on a tray. Minnie toddles out of the bedroom, races toward them, arms pumping. "Mama!" she squeals as she grabs Lena's shawl, almost knocking the baby from her arms.

"No!" Lena is surprised at the sharpness of her voice. "Be careful!" She steps back and leans down as Minnie begins to whimper. "See," she pulls the blanket away. "Baby."

Minnie stares for a moment. "Babeee." She reaches out and jabs the baby's cheek with her finger.

"No!" Lena jerks Sol away.

A crimson flush spreads over Sol's face as he begins to howl, and Minnie joins in. "Babee!" she hollers.

Lena carries Sol over to the armchair and crumples into it. He wails as she struggles to get him to take her nipple. Minnie yells louder and Lena grits her teeth as Sol begins to suck. "*Zolzein Sha*! Be quiet," she hisses at Minnie, who runs out, stomping her feet.

Later, when the baby sleeps, Lena sets him down and builds a fire in the stove. It's chilly, Morris will be home soon, and dinner has to be cooked. She leans on the sideboard, lightheaded. Her hands tremble as she pulls the dishes from the cupboard. She imagines dropping them and hearing the clatter as they smash to the ground, shards flying.

Morris is late, the chicken and rice are cold, and his breath smells like whiskey and cigars. Lena turns her head when he leans over her to touch the baby's face. Minnie races over to Morris. "Da-Da!" she hollers as he lifts her, rubbing his stubbly face on her cheeks as she giggles. Lena remembers when he used to kiss her, want her. It seems long ago.

She knows he'll go out again, stumble home before dawn, snore until late morning, then go off to work at the tailor shop, grumbling. She cradles Sol against her chest with one arm, as she wipes the table with the other. Morris puts on his hat and walks out the door without a word.

When Lena falls into bed she pulls Sol close and shuts her eyes. Minnie has fallen asleep on the bed next to her in her crumpled clothes and wet diaper. Lena begins to drift and dream as Sol roots into her bosom. She wakes when she feels damp curls in her face. Startled, she sees that Minnie has rolled over onto the baby, and she shoves her away. Minnie wakes and calls out, "Mama!" Sol wakes and howls. Minnie toddles over to where her old cradle hangs from a hook on the ceiling, climbs into it and demands, "Rock, Rock!"

"You're too old for that!" Lena hisses, but Minnie shrieks until Lena slides over from the bed, reaches out and swats the cradle. It swings, then slows, and she calls, "Rock Minneee!" until Lena pushes it again, over and over.

Before morning the door slams as Morris comes in and stumbles onto the couch. Minnie wakes again and hollers; Lena gets up, sits in the chair by the cradle, nursing Sol while she rocks Minnie back and forth, swinging harder. As winter light sifts into the room, there is a dull quiet and she leans back, dreaming in the chair. When she wakes, Minnie is standing and tugging on her shawl. Lena gasps as the baby nearly slips from her lap. She imagines his soft head hitting the floorboards.

Minnie starts to climb into the cradle again. "Rock Minnee!" she orders. Lena grabs her and pushes her away. She feels a bubble in her chest rising, like she is going to scream, but she keeps her mouth shut. Her hands find the fire poker from the stove; she swings it over her head, and strikes the cradle. Minnie backs into the corner and hollers, "Kaadull!" And then there is no sound. No air. Lena yanks the poker backward and pounds the cradle again and again, smashing it into pieces that crash to the ground in a heap. Minnie sucks in her breath and lets out another yowl, Sol wakes and cries, and Lena falls to the floor. She holds a piece of the cradle in her hand and pounds it into the ground, but her lips are silent.

The next evening as I drive Rachel to a friend's house in the fading light, a possum waddles in front of the car. There's just an instant before I pound the brakes and then a slow, grinding bump that seems to go on and on as we roll over it.

"I can see it flopping and wiggling like a worm!" Rachel is in tears. Behind us I see the skinny tail flapping up and down as it struggles to get out of the street.

Rachel screams, "MOM! Go back and hit it again so it won't keep suffering!"

I picture myself driving back up the street like a maniac and ramming it again. "I just can't do that," I tell her.

We stare silently as it squirms out of the road and into the woods. "Maybe it'll be okay," I say, but we know it won't. It will die a slow death somewhere, like Bubbe, squirming downstairs.

The next afternoon after I drop Ari off at a birthday party near the Rogue River, I have an urge to drive to the Table Rocks, the low, flat mesas that watch over the Rogue Valley. The impulse pulls me down country roads till I stop just below the Table Rocks, in a meadow. As the daylight fades, I walk slowly through the brush, while two hawks swoop down and glide dreamily over my head. It's very still in the last moment before the sun slips behind the mountain.

I start to weep. I want to feel the sky and the mountains and the hugeness of it all. I need to breathe big air, but I'm so trapped inside the walls of Bubbe's room that every breath I take is filled with her scent, no matter where I go.

After we hit the possum last night, words from the Talmud ran through my head, "*Do not do to others that which is hateful to you. Go and learn it.*" I did not mean to hit the possum. And my mother did not mean to abandon my sisters or me. She did the best she could, as I do with my own kids, but I know I've unknowingly hurt them. More than anything I want to teach them to listen to their own voices, but it's hard for me to be still long enough to hear my own voice. When I walked into the woods this evening I was frightened, thinking, "A woman isn't safe out here alone," but I was really afraid of the quiet beauty, the sound of my own heart beating.

I sit down by the stream and close my eyes. A picture of a mythic crone washing her clothes in the river drifts through my mind. I watch her swaying, dipping gray cloth into the water. "*When will my Bubbe die?*" I ask. She doesn't answer but stares back at me with dark eyes that have the river swirling in them. Then I imagine the worn out skin of Bubbe's body floating like a stretched, empty sack before the water carries it away.

Passover is coming next week. In my car, driving home from the middle school, I find myself singing, to the tune of "Go Down Moses," at the top of my lungs, "LET MY BUBBE GO!"

I keep trying to go to Ari's soccer games, teach three classes, get physical therapy for my shoulder, keep the house in order, be lovers with David, get along with my rebellious twelve-year-old and be there for my intense fifteen-year-old, all while what's really going on in my life is: Bubbe is dying downstairs.

On Saturday afternoon Karen asks me to come downstairs while she takes a break. She likes to walk Charlie on the wooded trail above our house. When he sees Karen coming with the leash, Charlie jumps up and spins around, barking wildly. As I walk down into Bubbe's room I'm struck by a new odor. Since Bubbe pulls her diaper off now, Karen lets her lie on a pad, then changes the pad. The air is warm and foul with the sweet acrid smell of old urine. I settle into the easy chair across the room as Karen and Charlie charge down the driveway. Bubbe moans and coughs softly in her sleep. She sounds like a sick, cooing pigeon.

Grandpa Morris used to keep homing pigeons in their backyard in North Hollywood. My cousin Tommy would tie messages to their legs, take them a few miles away, then let them go to test their homing instincts. I remember a cacophony of soft, guttural cooing that mingled with the scent of magnolia trees.

Bubbe was in the kitchen then, making icebox cookies that she would shape into a roll, then set to cool in the refrigerator before she sliced them into thick bland wedges to bake. They tasted hard and plain, since she always cut the amount of sugar in half, and never used salt. "I dessn't eat salt," she'd say, or "I dessn't eat sugar," her eyebrows knotted into a look of sour resolution, as if to warn us that sweetness and flavor should be watched out for, vigilantly.

Now she lies in her bed cooing faintly, but the sound is mixed with the scent of decay and urine, not magnolias. She can no longer cook, or walk, or warn us about the lavishes of life. I pray that her homing instincts are good.

twenty-nine

At night I dream of Bubbe's gurgled breathing bubbling up from deep muddy water. I wake to remember that I'm still here with her, living and dying every day.

When I go downstairs today Marilyn pulls me into the kitchen.

"I have to have another day off." She tells me. "I'm exhausted.

I nod and try to explain again. "Ok, but It will have to be a whole twenty-four hour shift because I can't afford to hire someone for a shorter, daytime hours."

She glares at me. "That's not what I need."

I shake my head. She puts her hands on her hips and moves in closer. "Well, Karen has to learn to put the sheets in the laundry room before she leaves!" I nod, stare. She takes a pan from the sink. "She left macaroni burnt into this pot!" I want to say, "Stop! Macaroni doesn't matter." But it feels like the macaroni is burnt into me. Something is burning. I hear Bubbe babbling from her bed. The room is so hot and stuffy that I'm dizzy. Marilyn stares at me. I know she's exhausted. I know she's sad, too, watching Bubbe slip away. I want to tell her I'll try to help her, but my stomach feels sick and I can't breathe. Her voice is piercing. "The hospice aide didn't show up to bathe Bubbe and her toenails need to be clipped. . . You'll have to phone the agency. . . These cooking pots have aluminum. That's toxic!" I nod my head. It all feels toxic. "I'm doing the best I can, " I mumble, "I'm

166

doing what I can." Bubbe groans in her sleep and gasps for air, and I know there isn't enough air in this room for me and Bubbe and Marilyn and all the ghosts that hide under the dark paneling. I stumble back upstairs, sit down on the couch and breathe slowly, but the air still feels too thick.

Rachel races in. "I'm going to Nicole's and I need my red shirt! It's still in the dirty pile! Why didn't the laundry get done?"

I hear my voice, flat, dull. "Because . . . there's so much . . . dirty laundry from Bubbe's sheets . . . that I haven't done any clothes." Rachel stares at me, shrugs, and walks out.

I know I need to ask for more help, but my arms feel leaden, my voice muffled. I can't think. I can't think. David walks in. "Should we ask the Bornstein's to have the Seder at their house instead of ours? It's too crazy here." It's too crazy here. I start to laugh. We need a Seder, it means order. I can't find any order. I laugh harder. But it's a loud hollow laugh without air. Ha ha ha, a sneering laugh that has no beginning. David backs away.

"Where are you going?" I hear myself yelling at him. Then I'm crying. "I don't know where you're going, I don't know where you're going!" He comes back in and sits down. But I'm crying, then laughing, then sobbing, as if the screws of civility have come loose, flying around the room. I can't collect them. Put them in order. Seder, order. I want order. There is no order here. Bubbe is dying and living and I am dying and living, but I can't separate the two. I need sleep but I can't sleep.

Could I really be losing my mind? I can see David is scared and doesn't know what to do. I don't know what to do with me. One of us calls my friend Juli, who is a therapist. She comes over, sits on the bed and puts her arms around me, tells me it's okay to fall apart, tells me it will all be better once I get some sleep, and gives me a tranquilizer. She talks to me about options, "You could put Bubbe in a nursing home; you could use my office downtown for alone space". . ."You could do this . . . you could do that." The sound of her voice is soothing, caring, competent. Eventually I calm down and Juli leaves. David tucks me into bed very tenderly, so tenderly that we make love in sweet relief, and then I sleep.

I dream that I'm riding a bicycle in the dusk, uphill, then running in the dark. The terrain seems vaguely familiar, but I'm not sure where I'm going or whether or not I'll ever get there.

The next day I feel woozy, as if I'm covered in soft gauze stretched over a wound, and I don't know if it will hold together.

Bubbe is slipping into a daze. Her body radiates warmth, her bones seem sharp and hot, her eyes half-lidded. Her spit is thick green with dark red globs. She has stopped drinking fluids, stopped talking, and her eyes are tilted up to the ceiling. I sit down by her bed, and reach over to hold her hand.

"I Love you, Bubbe. I'm here." I say

Her eyes are open, but she stares past me.

I go out for a walk, knowing I need air, and my body needs restoration. I hike to the trail above our house, then slide off the path to a place where three trees come together. There's a flat notch between the trees where I sit sometimes when I need a quiet place to think, or to pray. I put my hands on the tree trunks and feel the cool sturdiness, then I silently call for Bubbe's mother, Rose, and my mother, Bernice. When I feel their presence, I say out loud, "Please help guide Lena out."

The next morning is the day before Passover. I've agreed to make chicken soup with *matzo* balls for the first night's Seder, even though we've moved the Seder to our friends' house. I'm alternately tending to the soup and helping Rachel sew piles of tote bags for a project for disadvantaged children that she got herself over-committed to.

The matzo crumbs blend with the eggs and oil until they form a soft grainy mixture like damp mortar. When I scoop up a handful I hear Bubbe's voice from long ago. *You dessn't peck dem too tight, or dey'll come out hard, like rocks.* I cradle the sticky mass in my hand, shape it gently into a loose ball, and place it on the plate. When they are all formed and the water is salted and boiling, I drop each one in gently, knowing they will be light and fluffy. Bubbe's *K'nedelach*, her matzo balls, were one of the few foods that she didn't overcook.

Downstairs Bubbe is in a trance. I've seen her come and go many times since she's been here, but this time there is no way back. The air is thick and sour in her room. She's spits clots of blood between breaths that sound as if she is desperately sucking through a clogged straw. Her half-opened eyes stare at nothing.

I sit with her for a time trying to sense the rhythm of her heartbeat, the little life she has left. I touch her arm gently until I see that she sees me.

"Do you know who I am?" I ask her.

"Debbie." She gurgles the word.

It's silent for a while, then I begin to stroke her arm and speak. "Passover is coming tomorrow, Bubbe. It's time to go out of Egypt. It's time. The Red Sea is going to part for you, Bubbe. Moses is going to lead you out of Egypt." She nods, flicks her eyelids, seems to hear. "It's okay for you to go now, Bubbe. We love you. We'll be fine, and we're going to remember you. Rachel and I are cooking chicken soup with *matzo* balls, just like you used to. And we're sewing, like you taught me. We're going to make popovers from your recipe all during Passover. We're going to always remember you. We love you, Bubbe. It's time to let go."

In the late afternoon Rachel comes downstairs to visit. She leans over and kisses Bubbe. Bubbe, who hasn't appeared to see anything or spoken any words in hours, musters a strained whisper. "How are you, honey?"

Rachel says, "I'm good, Bubbe. I love you."

"I love you too," whispers Bubbe, and these are her last words.

The Breath

Oxygen, carbon dioxide, greenhouse, rainforest, cycle, recycle, balance
The Breath
what is taken in
what is transformed by the heart
what is released
The Breath

- Earth Voices Deck, Robert Beridha

thirty

At seven-thirty in the morning there is a knock on our bedroom door. When I open the door, Karen says quietly, "She's gone."

David and I walk downstairs to see Bubbe exactly where we left her, on the left side of the bed, her eyes open, her mouth agape, her arm raised, but she's so utterly motionless that it's a shock. I keep expecting her to suddenly take a breath, like in a horror movie when the villain has been killed and it's dead quiet and suddenly he jumps up to scare the pants off you one last time. But she doesn't. She's gone.

For a few moments we just stand there because we're in the presence of death, because she has finally made it out of that body and the air is so still. I sit down on the edge of the bed and touch Bubbe's arm; it feels cool and hard. David, Karen, and I chant, "*Shema Yisrael, Adonai Elohenu, Adonai echod.*" Hear, oh Israel, the Lord our God, the Lord is one.

I begin to sing softly in Yiddish, "*Shluff mein Kin, Loo, Loo, Loo. . .*" I reach over to gently close Bubbe's eyes, but they slowly slide open again.

The day dissolves into phone calls and practicalities. It's decided that David will conduct the funeral in Los Angeles where Bubbe owns a plot. It has to be delayed for a couple of days because of Passover, so we'll fly in Tuesday for the service Wednesday morning. A man in a suit arrives to pick up the body and take it to the local funeral home until it's flown to Los Angeles. David and I help him lift her body onto a gurney that he covers with a pale sheet. Rachel and Ari are awake now, and they stand silently staring as Bubbe is wheeled out.

Later I nap a little, get up, drink some coffee, try to go on, but I can hardly move. I'm letting it sink into my pores: It's over. I lay my head down and weep.

In the afternoon I go to the funeral home for *Tahara*, the ritual washing of a dead body while prayers are said, a final cleansing. It's done by the *Hevre Kedisha*, a group of volunteers in our Jewish community. Family members don't usually participate, but since we helped to care for her so close to her death, Marilyn and Karen and I want to finish by preparing her body for the grave.

In the lobby of the funeral home are Jackie, the student Rabbi who will lead the rituals, Sue, who will read the prayers, Marilyn, Karen, three other women volunteers, and me. As Jackie talks with the funeral director, I remember Aunt Derril's words on the phone this morning when I called to tell her Bubbe had passed, *You did what I could not do.* I suddenly remember the amulet she sent to me a few months ago with writings from ancient Babylonian baskets. Instead of wearing it, I hung it over my bed. Now I realize it should go around Bubbe's neck, as a gift from her daughter, Derril.

I tap Jackie on the shoulder." I need to go home and get an amulet to put on Bubbe." I tell her.

Jackie hesitates."Well, we don't usually put things in Jewish coffins," she says. "It's not an Egyptian funeral." I see she's torn between doing what is *Halachic*, according to Jewish law, and serving the needs of the family.

"How long before we're ready?" I ask her.

"Ten minutes."

"I'll be back in eight. I need to do this." Jackie nods as I run out. I drive home, grab the amulet, race back. Seven minutes flat.

When I return, the women are standing outside the room where Bubbe's body is to be washed, and it's clear that this isn't an everyday gathering. There's an odd aura of apprehension. Jackie, who'll be getting the wettest, and Marge, are donning protective outfits. They pull them on in a silent staccato, until they look like aliens in yellow rubber raincoats, hooded, their eyes peering out. The rest of us put on surgical gloves and white plastic aprons tied neatly behind our waists. We look like we're lined up to go to a tea party.

I gather the women into a circle and thank them for coming. Jackie says, "We ask for the presence of the ancestors and *Shekhina*, the female presence of God, to guide us as we help lift Bubbe's soul to heaven." She gives us some final instructions before we enter the room silently.

Bubbe is laid out on a metal table with a sheet covering her, but the sheet fails to hide her awesome presence. It fills the room. We slowly take our positions around the table, Jackie at the helm. She pulls the sheet off and for a moment we gaze at the body. It is not every day that you look at any dead body, but this one is so entirely used up that it takes your breath away. Bubbe's eyes stare at us with a glossy-gummy sheen like old marbles. Her skin is yellowed and translucent. All of her bones seem huge, jutting, but the pelvis takes prominence, sitting like an ancient ark.

Jackie leads us in the ritual washing as we pour pails of water over each part of the body, turning it gently, this way and that. The runoff drains through holes in the metal table, dripping into a container below. The water feels icy, even through the gloves, and the room smells like cold death, latex, and talcum. The body slides heavily as the gloves squeak when we turn her, rinse her, turn her.

Sue reads the prayers aloud in Hebrew and in English. "You are pure, your face is like milk and honey, your body is a bouquet." It's hard to miss the irony here. Her body is old, decrepit, blood-smeared. She lived so long that she was actually rotting before our eyes.

Jackie hands me a cloth to wipe a blood smear from Bubbe's face. Her skin feels like chilled plastic under my gloves, so different from the fuzzy cheeks I touched yesterday. I comb her hair gently off her forehead. We chant over and over, "*Tahor*... she is pure... *Tahor*... she is pure... *Tahor*."

We're about to wrap her in the traditional white shroud, when I notice a little glob of feces has slipped from her bottom, kind of like the feces that sometimes slips out during childbirth. You can't really separate any of this stuff, not in birth or death or anywhere in between. We carry creation and destruction inside us, holiness and rottenness. Both are undeniable in this room. I motion to Jackie who hands me the cloth to do one last honor. *Tahor. . .* she is pure.

We wrap Bubbe in the shroud and twist the belt three times as Jackie instructs us. I sprinkle earth from Jerusalem over her as Sue leads the women in chanting. We wrap her head, and she looks regal, clean and shiny. Her cheeks no longer seem sunken; rather, her cheekbones look chiseled, strong and elegant. When I place the amulet from Derril around her neck, she looks like Queen Tut.

I tell the women, "My aunt Derril sent this unwittingly as a gift to her mother—she just misfired a little and sent it to me." I look around the circle and see many women who've had strained relationships with their mothers. "I dedicate this mis-sent amulet to the connections between mothers and daughters, especially the painful ones." Everyone nods. "May those relationships continue to heal in unexpected ways, like this time with Bubbe has perhaps healed some of the wounds of the mothers and daughters in my family."

Jackie and I each take one side of Bubbe's stiff body and carefully lift her into her coffin. Marilyn places her "Teddy Bear" in with her. We close the coffin lid slowly as we pray for her spirit to soar on the wings of *Shekhina.*

Rachel, Ari, David and I travel light for the trip to Los Angeles, but my limbs feel heavy. I stare ahead at the front row of airline seats where I sat gripping Bubbe's hand five months ago, the two of us so frightened of the unknown. The front exit row is now eerily empty.

At the funeral home, friends and relatives crowd in. Cousin Tracy leans in and hugs me. "Thank God you got her out of that nursing home!" she says. Cousin Marcie stares at me and says, "How on earth did you do it?"

I shake my head. "I don't know," I tell her. "We just did."

David gathers us for the service with some songs and prayers, then reminiscing about Bubbe. Rachel stands up and tells about a secret code she and Bubbe had. She would say, "What's cookin'?" and Bubbe would answer, "Da beans is cookin' today," if she was feeling good. On a bad day, she'd say, "Nuttin's cookin', honey, not much cookin' today."

I talk about how sweet Bubbe was at the end, how she "outlived her personality." Then I hear myself say, "I felt like Bubbe's soul called out to me and I was lucky enough to be able to answer." The room is very still, but I see heads nodding.

As soon as we get home the house begins to shift into reverse gear as we get ready to inhabit our old spaces. When I go downstairs to scrub the rails of Bubbe's bed before the rental company comes to retrieve it, I realize I'm too tired to do it. I just sit down on the floor beside the bed and stare at the silhouette of the rails against the window. David walks in, sits down, and puts his arms around me. "I need some time off," I tell him, and he nods.

I call a cleaning service to come take care of Bubbe's room, then call a friend who has a cabin at a nearby lake to see if I can spend a couple of days there. I need to slow down and loosen the knots I've tied inside myself in the last months.

As soon as I arrive at the cabin, I collapse on the couch, then fall asleep. When I wake an hour later, I realize my whole body feels drained, the way my belly felt in the days after giving birth. Still swollen, but empty. I expected a revelation, or at least a new sense of peace after my ordeal with Bubbe, but it's not there yet. Even though Bubbe got to the other side, I'm not sure where I am. I make a sandwich and carry it out to the dock, where I sit and stare at the ripples on the lake while the sun sets.

The next morning I go for a walk around the edge of the lake until I find a little secluded cove, where I sit down to meditate. I follow the instructions from the meditation book I brought with me to quietly watch my feelings and thoughts, *breathe in, breathe out.* It's hard to be in the present moment when my whole being is still jumbled up in Bubbe's room, sifting through the scenes of our time together.

When I get up and amble down a path into the woods, I see a huge exposed root under the stump of an ancient tree. It looks like a gnarled, gruesome but glorious earth-mother. She is moss-covered, solid but delicate, ferns sprouting from her belly, branches beckoning. I move closer until I feel my skin against the moss and breathe in the deep fragrance. My body wants to to be held in her embrace, but something in me holds back. Mostly I feel the sharp ache of my longing.

I keep asking myself, *Did I do enough?* Of course I did enough for Bubbe, did everything I could. It's dawning on me, though, that I can never *do* enough to feel fulfilled. That is the hardest thing to look at. The place of loss and longing: the place where Bubbe's story forever spills into mine. When I leaned into the tree stump, I yearned for the simple, earthy love that flows from the bodies of mothers to their children. At the same time I sensed how that love was twisted in my family, as the rage from Rose filtered through Lena, shriveled her joy, and trickled like a polluted stream to my mother, my sisters, to me.

It would be nice if that cycle was finished, if Bubbe's visit brought a magical healing, but that would be a false ending. I do know something was altered, though, the angle shifted. It's not because anybody did anything, it's simply that we were able to let something happen. In the quiet moments when Bubbe and I stepped out of our stories and just breathed together, that was the magic. In the midst of all the turmoil, we found the surprising gift of tenderness.

When I drive back home in the afternoon I see the azaleas along our driveway have opened in a bright orange blaze, and the dogwood buds are a fuzzy pink, ready to burst into bloom. Inside the house is quiet as I walk slowly downstairs into Bubbe's room. The bed is gone and the room smells faintly of Lysol.

You can't begin to move on unless you're totally present in this moment, says the meditation book. But I can't be only in the present. I carry Bubbe with me in my bones, her strength as well as her sadness, and I'm as aware of her presence now as I am of my feet on the warm wool carpet, and the sun glinting in the window, lighting the space where her bed was yesterday.

I go into the bathroom and open the medicine cabinet to empty it of the last traces of Bubbe: a bottle of laxative pills, a toothbrush, and a little jar of ear drops. I drop them into the trash and close the mirrored cabinet door. For a moment I stare at my reflection in the glass until everything blurs and I see a faint image of Bubbe behind me, blended with my face. I speak to her in my mind. *We almost couldn't do it. It was so hard in the last few weeks that I thought I was going insane. But we all lasted, Bubbe. We got you home.*

epilogue

Yesterday I emailed my daughter Rachel, who is now 32 years old, to tell her I was tempted to come visit her and my three-year-old granddaughter in Virginia because they needed some extra help this month. She replied gently, "It's ok mama, stay home and finish your book that has been seventeen years in the making."

It's true. I've worked on this memoir on and off for seventeen years, scrapping together moments for an undertaking that I could not let go of, despite a busy life and an ambivalent relationship with the writing that terrified me. As a storyteller I'm aware that stories make concentric circles within and around our lives, tracing the conscious and the subliminal, while carving our hearts with unseen force. Just as I was compelled to bring my grandmother to my home despite knowing it would rattle my whole family, I was driven to write this story because I knew it was a big story, standing out like a relief map against the smaller tales of my everyday life. At Bubbe's funeral I said "I feel like her soul called out to me, and I was lucky enough to be able to answer." That sense propelled me through the experience and the subsequent painful discoveries that the telling of it would reveal.

After Bubbe died, a cousin said, "I wish I could have done what you did, but I hated her." Since Bubbe was such a difficult person before her dying months, other relatives echoed that sentiment in varying degrees, perhaps less bluntly. I'm not sure why I did not hate her. Being as grouchy and sensitive as anyone in the family, I'd been guilty of reacting angrily to Bubbe's negativity on countless occasions, but we shared an unspoken bond that surfaced during her time in my home. It took death to call us to that bond. Just as her core emerged while the husk of her body deteriorated, her passage from this world allowed me to sit with her in quiet moments of truth. When I said that Bubbe "outlived her personality" I meant that her crusty covering of negativity slipped away, allowing a more luminous core to emerge. The only word I have for that core is soul.

In a famous Hasidic story, a prince goes under the table, takes off his clothes and munches on grain, convinced he is a rooster. A wise man cures him by going under the table, taking off his clothes, and munching on grain with him. In other words, he meets the prince exactly where he is, gains his trust, then gradually leads him to self-awareness and eventual return to the outer world. The story illustrates what I struggle with daily in meditation: meet yourself where you are. If the goal in meditation is to show up and accept yourself exactly as you are, the key element in a good death may be meeting the dying person on their own terms. Just as each life is unique, so is each death. When I let go of expectations of Bubbe's "perfect death," I was able to take off my metaphoric clothes and crawl under the table with her.

Although I had vague notions of helping Bubbe to resolve some of her difficult past, perhaps even to forgive her mother and forgive herself, that was clearly not what happened. It was I who needed to examine the past. The long journey of writing the memoir allowed me to sift through the family toxins so I could feel my sadness, see the stories through a wider lens, and move on. I began the journey by saying yes to Bubbe's call to accompany her through the passage of death, but the surprising aftermath was allowing the stories to light my own path home.

I've been asked, "Would you do it again?" Faced with the harrowing parts of the experience, people wonder if they could withstand the rigors of tending to a death while living with a family. It's a fair question. Not every death belongs at home, and not every family is equipped to deal with it smack in the center of their lives. Personally, I've learned to say "No" more often as I age. When I screw up the courage to turn down a request (*could you volunteer to tell one more story, can you host another dinner for congregants*) I consider it a victory for self-preservation. But to Bubbe, I would say yes again without hesitation. I've learned that no matter how grouchy, selfish, overwhelmed or imperfect we are, we can still be called to something important. A soul can wake up another soul to show up for moments of grace. I am forever grateful to Bubbe for that.

discussion questions

1. Why do you think Debra decided to bring Bubbe out of the nursing home to her house, despite all her misgivings? At the funeral Debra says, "I feel like her soul called out to me and I was lucky enough to be able to answer?" What do you make of that?

2. What do you think of Debra's handling of her teenage children? Do you think Rachel and Ari were shortchanged by the focus being on Bubbe while their mother was overwhelmed, or were they enriched by the experience? To what extent should children living at home get to have input and responsibilities?

3. Debra has difficulties with the caregivers, especially Marilyn, the primary caregiver, and she wishes she could be more patient and sensitive to the caregivers' needs. What do you think of how she dealt with these issues, and how do you think you might handle having caregivers living in your home?

4. Bubbe was described as being a difficult, negative person throughout most of her life, but she became more kind and friendly in her last months. Debra says, "She outlived her personality." This happens sometimes in the last stages of life, but sometimes it is just the opposite. Have you experienced someone in the last stages of death? How were they changed before their death?

5. How did being Jewish affect Debra and her family's decision-making? What did you learn about Judaism from this book?

6. Debra was resentful of her husband's lack of involvement in the care of Bubbe. Was she justified in her feelings? Most home caregiving in U.S. is done by women. Was this situation just typical of that dynamic? How did her feelings toward David's involvement change as she became more aware of her own feelings of abandonment by her mother?

7. The story of Bubbe's stay at the Zaslow's home is interspersed with stories from the past, that get more and more difficult as we discover Bubbe's history of abuse. What was the value of delving into the difficult family stories? Did they change your view of Bubbe, Debra, or the family?

8. Death. Family dynamics. Alcoholism. Intergenerational cruelty. What do you think this book is really about? Does one theme take prominence over the others for you?

9. In the Epilogue, Debra says, "Not every death belongs at home, and not every family is equipped to deal with it smack in the center of their lives." Would you want to bring your parents or other relatives into your home when they're unable to take care of themselves? Would they want that? What considerations, physical, emotional, intellectual and spiritual, might guide decision-making for yourself and others?

10. If you have a life partner, is there agreement about how to proceed in your lives when it comes to elders for whom you might have responsibilities or guardianship at some point? What might help you discuss this together?

acknowledgements

This project could not have been completed without the help of numerous people: My instructors at Vermont College of Fine Arts, especially Larry Sutin and Sue William Silverman; my MFA buddies, especially Kathryn Kay and Lyssa Tall Anolik; my writing group, especially Debra Murphy and Jennifer Margulis, who offered continual incisive feedback; my women's group, Laurel Miller, Rachael Resch and Sharon Dvora, who cheered me on; Pat Florin, whose copy-editing made the manuscript shine; Robert Beridha, who offered his "Earth Voices" deck and unwavering friendship; Jan Jacobs, whose coaching genius helped me stay on track year after year; and finally, Steve Scholl and the crew at White Cloud Press who brought the book into being.

Mostly I want to thank my family: David, Rachel, and Ari, for their constant loving support, and allowing themselves to be written about so intimately.

The events in the memoir are as I remembered them, although some scenes have been put in a different order for clarity. The scenes in Russia and Minnesota have been re-imagined based on my memory of my grandmother's telling. A few names have been changed for privacy.

My deepest gratitude, of course, goes to Bubbe for offering me the surprising gift of sharing her journey.

about the author

 DEBRA GORDON ZASLOW travels nationwide performing and leading workshops in storytelling and memoir writing. She holds an MFA in Writing from Vermont College of Fine Arts. Her specialty of Jewish folktales combined with personal narrative, and strong female heroines, is featured on her CD, "Return Again: Jewish Stories of Renewal and Transformation." She lives in Ashland, Oregon, where she teaches storytelling at Southern Oregon University, leads memoir-writing courses in the community, and runs a "Maggid" training program in Jewish storytelling with her husband, Rabbi David Zaslow. They have two grown children, and the cutest grandbaby in the world.